CONTENTS

DISCLAIMER

The content in this book is solely for personal growth and education. In the event of any physical distress, please consult with appropriate professionals. The information and the application of any protocols in this book is the choice of each reader, who assumes full responsibility for his or her understandings, interpretations, and results. The author assumes no responsibility for the actions or choices of any reader. No part of this publication may be reproduced, stored in a retrieval system, or transmitted in any form or by any means, electronic, mechanical, photocopying, recording or otherwise, without the written permission of the author.

The authors of this book do not dispense medical advice or prescribe the use of any technique as a form of treatment for physical, emotional, or medical problems without the advice of a physician, either directly or indirectly. The intent of the authors is only to offer information of a general nature to help you in your quest for mental, emotional, and spiritual well-being. In the event you use any information in this book for yourself, the author assumes no responsibility for your actions.

c2024 - J.J & Tamo

ISBN 9798322057864

*"**To the ones who disobey tyranny and work on themselves
to become a better version than the day before**."*

"**Education is not preparation for life, education is life itself.**" - John Dewey

AUTHORS' NOTE

This book contains a wide variety of topics which can be useful to the reader at the appropriate time according to each individual's level of knowledge and understanding of themselves and life. Feel free to start reading anywhere in the book. We all are at different levels of understanding and emotional states at any given moment.

If a specific chapter/topic does not interest you, leave it for a later time. One example for what we're trying to point is, *you didn't feel like eating a specific meal when your parents cooked sometimes, but you did eat the same kind of food at another time*. The same applies here, take your time, do not rush. Absorb, take it in, breathe and let it go. Everything is useful in its own appropriate time. Do not read just for the sake of reading. Follow your intuition and your heart. Question everything and practice/experiment what you learn. You are your own best scientist and teacher. Life is not complicated. We make it complicated through overthinking. It is better to be a jack of all trades, master of none rather than master in one area in life and lacking a lot on everything else. The best way is to be a master of everything, but that will require countless of lifetimes. And you are not required to be a master of everything in this lifetime. At least not as long as you have a physical body.

Your body is both your paradise and your hell. What you do with it, will determine which state you are going to be living your life in, in a state of clarity and empowerment or a state of confusion and defeat.

P.S. All books from other authors mentioned throughout this book, are books that we got on Amazon. The reason we are mentioning this is that most of these books are only available for purchase on Amazon. This way you know where to look first for any of the books that you may be interested to read. There is a reason for everything. Just as there is a reason (a spiritual one) why you are reading this one at this time.

P.P.S. Countless of quotes are rightly or wrongly attributed to different teachers, authors, mystics, phylosophers etc. What matters is the message. No real truther or wise person would care for fame or recognition. On social media many times, people wrongly get angry or end up arguing with each other about who's certain quote is attributed to. I have news for you - All knowledge belongs to us. If for example, we create a quote and many people share it, is that quote/

knowledge ours (this book's authors' quote)? No, it is not.

What we think and write here (beside the quoted parts from other books/authors) in this book or anything we say throughout our daily life is simply a compilation of knowledge from other authors, coworkers, family members etc. So, if we were to trace back who said what, we would end up at the source of everything which is ourselves. We are the authors of everything, we are the manifestation of the Great One. All of this is to emphasize the importance of not getting attached to any name, person or ideology.

The importance of mentioning other books or wise people is so that the reader is exposed to more streams of knowledge and understanding. I have read a few books that didn't mention any other authors. Yes, I learned a few things from those books but thats it, I was met with a dead end. The authors of those books were not wrong. All I am saying is that we (the authors of this book) prefer to mention other people's work/books so that you as a reader, when you are done reading this book, you can look up the books/authors that we have mentioned here. Also we thank individuals who we don't know their names, who unknowingly to them, helped us with their thoughts/opinions

Rebuild Yourself From

WITHIN

THE PATH TO
SELF-TRANSFORMATION

J.J & TAMO

1

FOOD QUALITY EQUALS LIFE OR DEATH

IT IS OF PARAMOUNT importance that you know and innerstand what to eat. The most important aspect of food is how it affects the PH (Power of Hydrogen) of the body. Foods are divided into two categories: Foods that have an acidic reaction in your body and foods that have an alkaline reaction. It is not necessarily related to the PH of the food itself. Alkaline foods are great detoxifiers, they will detoxify the body. The more alkaline a food is, the greater the detoxification that will happen in your body. Fruit is one of the best alkaline detoxifiers. Alkaline food is your body's best friend. Acidic foods slow, inhibit and stop the detoxification process. Acid-forming foods are inflammatory and mucus-forming, ultimately causing organ failure.

Acids can become free radicals causing tissue damage unless linked to an antioxidant (alkaline) and removed. So, if you consume mostly acidic foods, the few alkaline foods that you consume will not be able to remove all the free radicals as the acids are in a much greater number. Disease is a chemical imbalance, simple as that. The moment the body goes below alkaline levels specifically below the 7HP, that's when disease begins. Food such as fruit and vegetables are chemicals, but good and natural chemicals that are meant to be processed by your body and not lab created poison that is rampant everywhere. What you breathe and what you eat affects and regulates the whole body. The five major organs are important that they remain healthy. Many people are walking toward their grave and they don't even know it.

Their organs are rotten, even if at first glance they don't show it. The body fights with all it has to keep the five organs operational so they can function at a minimum. Eventually the body gives up and disease/death begins the final stage. Technically the person gives up, not the body. The body has already let the person know about the problem throughout life by giving many hints to the person.

> "The consideration of man's body has not changed to meet the new conditions of this artificial environment that has replaced his natural one. The result is that of perceptual discord between man and his environment. The effect of this discord is a general deterioration of man's body, the symptoms of which are termed disease". – Hilton Hotema

The five major organs are the five captains.

THE FIVE CAPTAINS

Heart
The heart is called the chief of the vital organs. Your heart regulates other organs by controlling circulation of the river of life or "blood." Your heart houses the spirit. It governs moods and mental clarity. The condition of the heart's health is shown by the colour of the face and tongue. When the colour of the tongue and face is dark red, it indicates excess, when it's pale grey it indicates deficiency. The heart is paired with the small intestine, which separates the pure from the impure by-products of digestion, controlling the ratio of liquids to solid wastes, and absorbs nutrients, which it then sends to the heart for circulation throughout the body.

Liver
The liver stores and enriches blood and regulates the amount of hormones released into the bloodstream for general circulation. When humans move physically, blood moves, when a human is still (sleeping), blood returns to the liver. This statement accords precisely with the established medical fact that during periods of rest, especially in cold weather, 30-50% of the body's blood supply collects in the liver and pancreas. During sleep, blood is fortified in the liver for use by the rest of the body during activity.

The liver houses the human soul (Hun), as reflected in the Chinese term hsin-gan (heart and liver), which means sweetheart or dear. The heart and liver house the most distinct human attributes. The liver is the body's metabolic headquarters, and it is directly responsible for a person's overall health and vitality. Liver conditions are reflected in the eyes, fingernails, toenails, and muscles. The liver's partner is the gallbladder, whose intimate functional relationship with the liver is well recognized by western medicine.

Pancreas

The pancreas controls the production of vital enzymes needed for digestion and metabolism. This function links it directly with its paired Yang partner, the stomach. If the pancreas fails to produce sufficient enzymes, digestion in the stomach stagnates, causing food to ferment and putrefy instead of digesting. The pancreas controls the human attribute of rational thought. Its dysfunction is reflected by emaciation of the skin, flesh, limbs, poor muscle tone, chronic fatigue, stagnant digestion, and the inability to concentrate.

Kidneys

The kidneys control water. Excess water and fluids are sent to the kidneys and converted into urine, which then are passed down to the bladder for excretion. Thus, the bladder is functionally linked to the kidneys as their hollow Yang partner. The kidneys are the gate of life because they control the overall balance of vital fluids in the body, which in turn directly influences energy level and balance. The kidneys are the major balancers of Yin and Yang in the human body. They house the human attribute of willpower and control the marrow, loins, and lumbar, and sacral regions.

Their dysfunction is often indicated by lower back- pain and the inability to straighten the spine. They are closely connected with the adrenal cortex (suprarenal glands), which straddles them and secretes cortisone, adrenaline, and vital sex hormones into the blood stream. The kidneys and their related glands thus control sexual function and potency.

Lungs

Lungs control Chee/life force energy, state Chinese medical texts. Since Chee means "breath" as well as "energy," the lungs govern both breathing and energy circulation. When breath is deficient, so is energy. The Yin lungs are associated with the Yang large intestine. Lung conditions are reflected in the skin, a fact well known to Western medicine, for the skin itself is a respiratory organ. Both the lungs and the large intestine are actually internal extensions of the skin, one pushed down from the top, and the other up from the bottom. Pneumonia and other severe respiratory ailments are generally accompanied by constipation, and constipation usually causes distension and discomfort in the chest.

STRESS weakens your heart and brain
FEAR weakens your kidneys
GRIEF weakens your lungs
ANGER Weakens your liver
WORRY Weakens your stomach

Your emotional, mental and physical health is in direct proportion of the quality of what you drink, eat and think. Alkaline foods are the best way to get you back to real health. A lot of people think they are healthy but if they took a good look at themselves they'd realize that they have been lying to themselves. Because we eat better then before it doesn't mean that we are healthy, it means that we are less sick. When you think like this you are pushed to do better.

> "If your blood is formed from eating the foods I teach [fruits and green-leaf vegetables] your soul will shout for joy and triumph over all misery of life. For the first time you will feel a vibration of vitality through your body [like a slight electric current] that shakes you delightfully". Arnold Ehret

Anything that obstructs the circulation of breath, nerves, blood, lymph and bowels inflicts a great deal of damage upon our human temple. The states of bad health, enervation and old-age are merely symptoms of a slow and miserable decline toward premature death. To improve the condition and capacity of our mind and body we must embrace Godly (divine/natural) habits and live in harmonious environments.

To cultivate good health, vitality, youthfulness and long life we must remove the causes of obstructions in the human temple by eliminating destructive conditions and clear existing obstructions from the human temple to improve its circulation. To clear existing obstructions, we must increase exposure to fresh air, pure liquids (filtered water, home made fruit juice, urine=structured plasma filtrate water), living foods (nothing cooked, or packaged store-bought food), and harmonious energy.

To optimize health, vitality youthfulness and longevity, it's crucial to shift our focus from building 'immunity' to enhancing the circulation of breath, nerves, blood, lymph and bowels. Improving bodily circulation, in essence, means cleansing and unblocking these interconnected channels. When one channel has blockages, it causes stagnation, adversely affecting the rest and leading to bad health. Crossing the body's threshold of tolerance by neglecting to cleanse these channels results in declining health, enervation, accelerated aging, and premature death. The path to robust health begins with this realization.

It involves a two-pronged strategy; firstly, removing the causes that lead to obstructions in each channel, and secondly, clearing existing blockages from each channel. You cant remove toxicity out of your body while eating at the same time, no matter how healthy you eat. Which means that fasting is a must so that the body is able to expel the accumulated filth over a long period of time. And only then will the body be able to heal properly.

Bibliography

Natural Treasure by Blake Cyrier

Body Mind Soul by Saimir Kercanaj

The Tao Of Health, Sex and Longevity by Daniel P. Reid

2

ALKALINE PLANT-BASED DIET

"No disease, including cancer, can exist in an alkaline environment" - Dr. Otto Warburg

AQIYL ANIYS STATED in his book ALKALINE PLANT BASED DIET that the Western reductionist paradigm reinforced the notion that if science hadn't given its stamp of approval, then the idea was not worth much. The problem was there was little science being done to uncover the benefits of plant foods, and most of the studies done were industry driven and promoted the consumption of animal and processed foods.

Dr. Sebi's methodology supports the idea that illness begins where the mucous membrane of organs has been compromised. The constant consumption of acidic foods, meat, dairy, and processed foods deprives the body of minerals, acidifies the body, and leads to development of chronic inflammation. This causes the over production of mucus and compromises organs' protective mucous membrane. The combination of reactions in the body provides an environment hospitable to disease because it paralyzes white blood cells. This allows for the proliferation of pathogens and leaves weakened organs susceptible to the pathogens.

The Western medical point of view looks at disease as being infected with a virus, bacteria, or fungus. People constantly encounter viruses, bacteria, and fungus, but that doesn't mean a person necessarily has to become sick. This means that pathogens are not the reason themselves that lead to illness. Sickness occurs when the body's natural defenses are not enough to keep it from succumbing to pathogens.

Western medicine uses acidic and unnatural chemicals to kill the pathogens that undermine organ health, instead of focusing on what the body needs to fortify its own natural defenses. Susceptibility to disease will remain when the integrity of organs and the immune system are weakened. Western pharmaceutical medicine is designed to attack specific pathogens, but its medicine sets up conditions that further undermine the integrity of organs.

It is essence, Western medicine's approach keeps the body in a constant state of internal weakness, leaving it susceptible to future pathogens. Sickness sets in when the pathogens can penetrate organs and disrupt cell function. The role of the mucous membrane is to protect organs by producing mucus to trap and neutralize pathogens for their removal from the body. Dr. Sebi explained if the mucous membrane in the lungs was compromised, the resulting illness would be pneumonia. A compromised mucous membrane in the bronchial tubes would result in bronchitis. In the pancreas, the result would be diabetes.

In the joints, the result would be arthritis. The consumption of meat, dairy, and processed foods acidifies the body, causes chronic inflammation, compromises the mucous membrane, and results in susceptibility to disease and deterioration of organ function. The body responds to heavy milk consumption and its toxins with increased mucous production and inflammatory processes to combat the threat. Casein, a protein in milk, has been linked to an increased risk of developing cancer. Casein consumption has also been implicated in the overproduction of mucus in the gut and respiratory glands.

Continuous consumption of meat and processed foods also compromise the mucous membrane because of the chronic acidic environment they develop. An acidic environment in the blood supports the proliferation of disease by shutting down white blood cells. Dr. Marcial-Vega, a renowned oncologist trained at Johns Hopkins University, gave a perfect example of this. Through his studies, he realized that an acidic environment wreaked havoc on the immune system and aided in the proliferation of disease.

Dr. Marcial-Vega examined the blood of his cancer patients and found red blood cells lost hemoglobin, became anemic, and clumped together to protect themselves against the acidic environment. This interfered with proper oxygenation of red blood cells and the delivery of oxygen to organs to support cell function. The acidic environment also paralyzed white blood cells, which allowed for uric acid and cholesterol and other toxins and pathogens to build up.

Dr. Marcial-Vega raised his patient's blood pH level to 7.4 simply by having them drink **GOJI-BERRY JUICE**. He used goji-berry juice at the time because he found it was the quickest natural way to turn the acidic environment of his patient's bodies into a slightly alkaline environment. The change helped to protect and strengthen their immune systems. The change to an alkaline environment allowed the red blood cells to separate and become properly oxygenated. This allowed for the proper delivery of oxygen and nutrients to organs to support healthy cell function. White blood cells woke up from their dormant state and could seek and neutralize uric acid, cholesterol, and other harmful organisms.

DR. MARCIAL-VEGA'S PATIENTS EXPERIENCED THE FOLLOWING WHILE PARTICIPATING IN THE GOJI-BERRY EXPERIMENT:

Ninety percent of his patients had a reversal of acidity to alkalinity. Eighty-five percent of his obese patients experienced significant weight reduction with an increase in lean body mass (no loss of muscle). Eighty percent maintained constant levels of hemoglobin, platelets, and white blood cells. That was significant considering cancer patients undergoing cancer treatment usually experience an 80–100 percent drop in these blood levels.

Eighty percent of his patients with high blood pressure experienced a drop in their blood pressure. Fifty percent had to decrease or eliminate their high-blood-pressure medication. Seventy-five percent of all his patients experienced an increase in libido. Sixty-seven percent of his patients with high cholesterol experienced a minimum drop of fifty points in four weeks. Sixty-four percent of his diabetic patients experienced a decrease in blood-sugar levels.

Dr. Marcial-Vega's experiment supported Dr. Sebi's position that an acidic environment supported the proliferation of disease and undermined organ integrity. His treatment also supported the notion that alkaline foods were supportive of the immune system and that they created an environment that was inhospitable to disease.

"It is the food that you eat that would reconnect you with the energies of life, and then the words are unnecessary because you

could see. You're connected." ~ Dr. Sebi

ALKALINE BLOOD AND THE ROLE OF PH

Aqiyl Aniys stated that Dr. Sebi's African Bio-Mineral Balance methodology introduced him to the concept that an acidic body supports the proliferation of disease, and an alkaline body protects against disease. The issue is a bit more complex, which gave people who wanted to be divisive ammunition to attack his methodology. More specifically acidic blood supports the proliferation of disease. Science supports the idea that there are alkaline parts of the body and acidic parts.

Stomach: Has a pH of 1.35 to 3.5, but the "Mucous Neck Cells" that are right below the surface of the stomach ling have a neutral ph.

Skin: The outer layer has a pH around 4 to protect it from the bacteria in the environment and the inner layer has a pH around 6.9.

Vagina: Has a pH around 4.5 to protect against microbial overgrowth.

Pancreas: PH is between 8 – 8.3.

Intestines: Small intestine has a range of 6-7.4pH, and the large intestine has a pH range of 5.7 -6.7.

Blood: Has a pH range between 7.35 and 7.45 (7.4 is the number commonly used).

> *Acid and alkaline are opposite sides of the pH scale. The scale for pH ranges from 0pH to 14pH. 0pH represents the highest acidic level, and 14pH represents the highest alkaline level. 7.0pH is neutral.*

Though different areas of the body are acidic it is very important to eat alkaline foods to maintain a blood pH around 7.4. The pH of the blood is the reference point for homeostasis, or optimal functioning of the organs in the body. The body works diligently to keep the blood in a slightly alkaline state near a pH of 7.4 to support homeostasis and health. pH stands for "potential hydrogen" and is the ability of molecules to attract hydrogen ions.

Too many hydrogen ions floating around the bloodstream makes the blood acidic and interferes with the proper oxygenation of cells in the body. Eating meat, dairy, processed foods, and even highly hybridized starchy plant foods acidify the blood because of their molecule structure. They also lack vital minerals, vitamins, and phytonutrients the body needs to properly perform metabolic functions.

The body uses oxygen to release energy from nutrients so cells can use components from the nutrients to heal, repair, and sustain themselves. Without the required energy, organ function is compromised, resulting in sluggishness and illness. An acidic environment wreaks havoc on the immune system's white blood cells and causes them to go into a dormant state. This allows bacteria, viruses, and fungi to proliferate, attack weakened organs, and interfere with normal and healthy bodily functions.

The pH of the blood sets the stage for the health of the whole body. When the body doesn't get enough alkaline material to maintain a blood pH around 7.4, the body will leach alkaline material from other areas of the body to maintain homeostasis. For example, the body will leach calcium from bones, at the expense of bones, to maintain the proper pH in the blood.[79], [80], [81] This leaching can lead to the development of osteoporosis and result in a reduction of bone density and bone fractures. The body uses buffering mechanisms, like the kidneys production of bicarbonate to maintain the desired alkalinity in the blood. When those systems are overwhelmed the body resorts to leaching alkaline material from fluids and tissues throughout the body.

The leaching compromises other areas in the body, leaving them susceptible to pathogens and toxins. The body will compromise other areas of the body because it is vitally important to maintain a blood pH around 7.4. Metabolic acidosis occurs when the pH in the blood drops below 7.4, which can result in stroke and death. The chronic consumption of acidifying foods compromises the health of the entire body and supports the manifestation of disease in any part of the body. Natural plant foods properly alkalize the blood and maintain its desired pH and support an environment that is inhospitable to disease. The consumption of natural plant foods optimally supports homeostasis or peak operation of organs.

Plants derive their nutrients from minerals they absorb from the earth, water, and air. Each type of plant is made up of different ratios and combinations of nutrients, which is determined by its genetic structure. Plant foods are loaded with micronutrients: minerals, vitamins, phytonutrients, and the carbohydrate macronutrient. These are the primary nutrients the body uses to support cell health and energy. Plants also contain fat, and nitrogen-based compounds called proteins, but in smaller concentrations. Meat, dairy, and processed foods on the other hand contain mostly fat and protein and are deficient in minerals, vitamins, phytonutrients, and carbohydrates.

The chemical structure of animal fat and protein also differ from plant fat and protein that alkalize the blood instead of acidifying it. Plants' minerals and vitamins help them to grow strong and vibrant, while plants' phytonutrients protect them against environmental pathogens. Plants absorb the sun's energy through the process called photosynthesis and convert its energy into physical forms of energy it uses for growth and to support chemical processes.

People consume the plants and absorb their natural balance of elements, compounds, and energy that are manifested in their minerals, vitamins phytonutrients, carbohydrates, fats, and proteins. As with plants, the human body is derived from these same elements and compounds. When people consume plant life, they consume elements and compounds that support the healthy function of organs. The chemical structure of natural plants has chemical affinity with the body, so their digestion doesn't produce harmful.

Meat, dairy, and processed foods are deficient in the minerals, vitamins, and phytonutrients necessary to support optimal organ function. The food industry was aware of the deficiency and developed vitamin and mineral supplements. Plant foods naturally provide nutrients in combinations the body recognizes, but artificial supplementation does not. Numerous studies have shown that vitamin supplementation increased mortality, while the nutrients in plant-based foods supported health.

A well-balanced, whole-food, alkaline plant-based diet is naturally high in minerals, vitamins, and phytonutrients. The diet is also high in natural carbohydrates which the body burns quickly for energy. Natural carbohydrates are the body's primary fuel source. The diet is also naturally low in fat and protein and provides a ratio of 80 percent carbohydrates, 10 percent fat, and 10 percent protein. This is the ratio nature provides to optimally support the healthy function of organs. An alkaline plant-based diet supplies the small amount of fat needed to support bodily functions, such as providing insulation for organs, storage of fat-soluble vitamins, and supporting brain function, growth, and cell functions.

It also supplies the small amount of protein needed to support antibody and enzyme production, transport of components, building and maintenance of cells, and transmission of messages throughout the body. The plant protein an alkaline plant-based diet provides fully supported the longstanding recommended daily allowance (RDA) of 10 percent protein. This was the recommendation for protein up until industry pressure influenced the Food and Nutrition Board to change the recommendation in 2002.

"A society that keeps cures a secret so they can continue to sell medication for huge profits is not a real society but a huge mental asylum." - Dr. Sebi

Sourced from *Alkaline Plant Based Diet* by Aqiyl Aniys

3

ALKALINE WATER RECIPE

"Alkaline water has become the most important advancement in health care since Penicillin" – Dr. William Kelly

The context of pH level

THE HUMAN BODY EXPERIENCES an ongoing exchange between blood, Cerebrospinal Fluid (CSF), sexual vital essences, and lymph. It is crucial to acknowledge that our eating habits directly impact these fluids.

Maintaining a pH level within the range of 7.35-7.45 is vital for the normal functioning of our cells, and a well-functioning body is proficient at achieving this balance:

– The body will experience metabolic alkalosis if the pH level exceeds 7.45.

– The body will experience metabolic acidosis if the value falls below 7.35

pH, short for potential hydrogen, represents the number of electrons (life force) accessible in the fluidic structure. When the pH is neutral or slightly alkaline, it signifies an abundance of free electrons in the body. Conversely, an acidic pH indicates an electron deficit within the organism.

The pH level of our body is significantly influenced by the acidity and alkalinity of the food we consume. Acidosis can manifest through symptoms such as headaches, lethargy, weakness, stiffness, fatigue, breathing problems, confusion, and anxiety.

In order to stabilize pH levels, the body extracts minerals (cell salts) like potassium, sodium, calcium, and magnesium from tissues to counteract acidity in the bloodstream. The kidneys play a crucial role in eliminating surplus acid from the body via urine, which highlights the immense effort required by these vital organs when our diets are excessively acidic. While our bodies possess remarkable mechanisms to regulate pH levels, it is our responsibility to support this process by nourishing ourselves with wholesome, alkaline-rich foods.

Animal products contain high levels of acidity, which can disrupt the natural balance in our bodies. By adopting a vegan diet, we can restore this balance and promote overall well-being. However, it is important to avoid overeating, consuming excessive amounts of processed acidic food, and indulging in alcohol, as these habits can hinder the development of our super consciousness.

"No drunkard can inherit the Kingdom of Heaven, for acids and alcohol cut, or chemically split, the oil (Christ Oil) that unites with the mineral salts in the body to produce the monthly seed" – George W. Carey

Context of Hydration

Adequate hydration is crucial; therefore, it is recommended to consume a sufficient amount of high-quality water. It is advisable to drink at least 3 liters of water per day. It is important to be cautious about the pH levels in bottled water and opt for water with a pH of 7 or higher. Furthermore, it is strongly advised to avoid consuming water that contains fluoride.

Water in its undisturbed environment (source) remains unaltered and possesses a high alkaline nature (typically with a pH level of 9 or above), along with an abundance of minerals. In this pristine condition, such water inherently aids in the preservation, rejuvenation, and revitalization of the body due to its elevated electron and mineral content.

As the human body consists of 70% water, one effective method to support the internal alchemical process is by promoting a neutral pH level within the body. This can be achieved by consuming water infused with alkalizing foods.

Given that the water we obtain from our taps and stores undergoes extensive processing, including distillation for purification and fluoridation, it has become exceedingly challenging to find water with a natural pH level of 9 or higher. Consequently, after conducting extensive research and experimentation, we have discovered that a blend of lemon, ginger, cinnamon, and pink Himalayan salt effectively enhances the quality of our water.

Water Recipe for Alkalizing Power

Specific quantities of each ingredient added to the water are not required. It is sufficient to thoroughly rinse the ingredients, then use a large jug or container to prepare the drink and store it in the refrigerator for future use.

Take a few lemons and slice them into quarters. Proceed to extract the juice from the lemons and pour it into your water jug. Furthermore, don't forget to incorporate the lemon peel into the water to enhance its taste.

1. *Lemon possesses potent antioxidant properties and enhances the immune system.*

2. *Lemons are alkaline-forming fruits that produce alkaline by-products during metabolism.*

3. *The aroma of lemon triggers the release of pheromones and oxytocin, which stimulates pineal metabolism.*

You have the option to either place a few Ceylon cinnamon sticks directly into your water jug or incorporate a few spoonfuls of powder. I utilize powder for the sake of simplicity.

Cinnamon enhances the sensitivity of insulin, which in turn promotes the expression of DNA genes.

Prepare a large ginger root by peeling and chopping it, then place the resulting pieces into your water. Alternatively, ginger powder can be utilized.

1. *Ginger enhances blood flow in the body.*

2. *Ginger acts as a potent antioxidant and cleanser of essential bodily fluids.*

3. *Ginger supports the purification of the endocrine glands, facilitating the distribution of nutrients to areas requiring healing.*

Incorporate 1-2 teaspoons of finely ground pink Himalayan salt into your water.

Salt acts as a conductor of electricity and has the potential to boost your piezoelectric charge. Nevertheless, standard table salt is devoid of numerous minerals that are abundant in Himalayan salt. Pink Himalayan Salt can also aid in regulating iodine levels in the body, which plays a vital role in generating ATP and energy, as well as kickstarting all essential bodily processes. Maintaining a proper iodine balance is crucial for fostering a beneficial bio-electrical vibration.

Insufficient iodine levels can have detrimental effects on our bodies. To put it simply, iodine is an indispensable, dynamic, and astonishing element. Nevertheless, it is important to conduct your own research as certain types of iodine can be harmful.

Iodine is widely distributed in the body, exhibiting antimicrobial, antibacterial, anti-mucus, anti-parasitic properties, while also supporting brain function, enhancing the immune system, and acting as an antiviral agent. Furthermore, it plays a role in the decalcification of the pineal gland.

Alkalinity and De-calcification

The accumulation of "lime scale" from fluoride and other calcifying agents can visibly affect showerheads and shower doors, just as acidosis and fluoride can lead to calcification of the body and pineal gland.

To maintain a long and healthy life, it is essential to keep the body's channels free from calcification. Consuming clean alkalizing foods, especially organic ones, helps in detoxifying the body and improving Pineal, Pituitary, and Thalamic functions. In a later chapter, we will discuss the importance of decalcifying the pineal gland for opening the third eye. The calcification of the pineal gland as stated above, is primarily caused by fluoride, a tool used by those who seek to control the planet through dark sorcery.

"The food you eat can be either the safest and most powerful form of medicine or the slowest form of poison" – Ann Wigmore

Bibliography

The sacred secretion by Kelly-Marie Kerr

4

BORN OF WATER AND SPIRIT

"The old texts of ancient wisdom say that in the supreme moment of metaphysical copula, the man and woman withdrew from the chemical copulation without ejaculating the semen. The sperm was considered sacred, and nobody in those times dared to profane sex" – Samael Aun Weor

To be born of water and spirit

UNDERSTANDING THE SIGNIFICANCE of baptism is crucial. Baptism symbolizes a commitment to sexual magic. If the child being baptized eventually honors the covenant of sexual magic, then the baptism is meaningful. However, if the child fails to uphold the pact of sexual magic, then what is the purpose of the baptism? Baptism on Epiphany in Eastern churches is tied to the marriage at Cana, while in Western churches, it is associated with Jesus' union with his church during epiphany. Therefore, baptism is linked to marriage and sex in both the east and the west, symbolizing a pact of sexual magic.

The effectiveness of baptism hinges on the fulfillment of sexual magic; without it, baptism loses its significance. I am sharing this with you to shed light on the esoteric importance of baptism. Within Christian churches, the baptismal font holds great significance as it represents the philosophical stone and the creative organs. The magnetized or lustral waters contained in the font symbolize the sacred sperm. To put it simply, water embodies the Mercury of secret

18

philosophy, while the fire from candles embodies the Sulphur of alchemy.

The second birth can only be achieved through Mercury, representing semen, and Sulfur, representing fire.

> *"The Semen is the astral liquid of man. In the semen*
> *is the Astral light"* – Samael Aun Weor

To Be Born Again: The Second Birth

The second birth signifies the emergence of the true human being. It is essential to bear in mind the profound words shared by Jesus with Nicodemus:

"Except a man be born of water and of the Spirit, he cannot enter into the kingdom of God."

The key to attaining the second birth lies in this fundamental aspect. However, the second birth cannot be accomplished without the creation of the superior existential bodies of the Being. These superior existential bodies cannot be brought into existence from nothingness, as nothing can emerge from nothingness. Therefore, the creation of the superior existential bodies of the Being must be based on Mercury and Sulfur.

Here in our rituals, we use the bread of transubstantiation to symbolize Mercury, the metallic soul of sperm, and the sacred wine to represent Sulfur, the fire of alchemy. It is essential to constantly mix Mercury and Sulfur within us to produce the superior existential bodies of Being.

Mastering all of this knowledge is essential in unraveling the mystery of the seal of Solomon. The upward triangle, representing Sulfur and fire, signifies the superior aspect. The lower triangle, which is connected to the upper triangle, symbolizes Mercury, indicating the sacred metallic soul of sperm.

After completing the magnificent labor, an extraordinary ring of divine essence is bestowed upon the individual in the celestial realm. This magnificent ring is always worn on the ring finger of the right hand. What is depicted on this ring? Solomon's seal. What does this seal signify? It signifies that the seeker has achieved the ultimate goal of obtaining the philosophical stone through the continuous amalgamation of Mercury and Sulfur.

By continuously combining Mercury and Sulfur, one can create the astral body. The next step involves creating the mental body, followed by the casual body. The possession of a physical body, an astral body, and a casual body automatically grants individuals their psychic spiritual principles, enabling them to truly embody the essence of being human, becoming an authentic human, a real human, a genuine human.

Upon attaining the second birth, one is considered to have truly become a human being. The first birth may have bestowed upon us the status of intellectual animals, but it is the second birth that grants us the privilege of being recognized as genuine humans. The continuous mixing of Mercury with Sulfur is symbolically depicted in the baptism ritual: the water symbolizes Mercury, while the fire represents the Sulfur used in alchemy.

The key to achieving the second birth and entering the kingdom of heaven after baptism lies in the intelligent combination of Mercury with Sulfur. Without working with these elements, baptism becomes meaningless. Thus, baptism is a pact of sexual magic. Throughout the ritual of baptism, it is widely believed that the serene white dove, representing the Holy Spirit, gracefully descends upon the child's head. This symbolism is deeply intertwined with the concept of the Holy Spirit embodying the same qualities as the enigmatic Mercury in the realm of secret philosophy.

Sulfur is essentially fire and should be interpreted as such. It is closely linked to Lucifer, which translates to "light-bringer" in Latin, similar to Prometheus. The presence of the Luciferic power (fire) within oneself is what gives rise to the sexual impulse. The power of Sulfur is undeniably extraordinary. Mercury alone is powerless, but once it is combined with Sulfur, or fire, it gives rise to the superior bodies of the Being. In its isolated state, Mercury lacks any inherent capabilities. Nevertheless, when Mercury is united with Sulfur, symbolizing fire, the resultant blend gives birth to the superior existential forms of the Being. Keep in mind that the Sacred Absolute Sun desires to solidify the three primary forces of nature and the cosmos within us, they are: Holy Affirming, Holy Denying, and Holy Reconciling.

Holy Affirming represents the positive force of the Father. Holy Denying embodies the negative force of the Son. Holy Reconciling symbolizes the neutral force of the Holy Spirit. In the eastern tradition, Brahma represents the Father, Vishnu the Son, and Lord Shiva the Holy Spirit. Within the realm of the secret philosophy, the Holy Spirit, symbolized by Mercury, takes form within us as we engage in the alchemical process of working with Sulfur and Mercury. However, this sacred work can only be conducted within the laboratory setting. It necessitates the precise combination of the different elements of Mercury and Sulfur, and this laboratory resides within the human organism.

"When you build up your semen and do not spill it carelessly, you are alchemically creating millions more microscopic phosphorus cells in your blood. This extra phosphorus equates to more chemical energy that rises up your spine via the twisting serpents, the central nervous system, that can then be best utilized for your brain" – Moe Bedard

Therefore, within our laboratory, we intelligently combine Mercury, the metallic soul of the sperm, with Sulfur. This combination yields a formidable outcome: the birth of the astral body in the humanoid as the first outcome, the birth of the Mental body as the second outcome, and the birth of the Casual body as the third outcome. Once one possesses these vehicles, the true human, born of Mercury and Sulfur, of water and fire, is born. This is the understanding one must have. That is why Christ said:

"Except a man be born of water and of spirit, he cannot enter into the kingdom of heaven."

We need to undergo a rebirth. Simply being born as intellectual animals is not sufficient; it is quite subjective. Now, we must be born as true humans, and a true human is born of Sulfur and Mercury, as is always emphasized in baptism.

Rules and measures govern everything in life. Justice, a sacred concept, is undeniably real. In ancient times, alchemists symbolized justice with a divine queen-like figure holding a scale in her left hand, adorned with weights to maintain balance. Standing on a philosophical stone, she dons a white robe beneath a regal purple mantle, crowned with gold. Notably, she wields a sword of justice in her right hand. The significance lies in the precise weights and measures of the cosmic justice scale, emphasizing the necessity for laboratory work to align with the law.

The specific proportions of Sulfur and Mercury that are blended together remain undisclosed to ordinary individuals, and even the alchemists themselves. These enigmatic details belong to the realm of nature's greatest secrets. Nonetheless, the alchemist's work is governed by the principles of justice, as justice serves as their guiding principle.

If an alchemist has a priestess-wife and decides to engage in sexual activity with another woman, he commits adultery. This is because two conflicting currents inside the dorsal spine clash, resulting in a short circuit that burns the sacred thread where the snake rises. Adultery is a serious offense in alchemy.

Fornication is another grave matter to consider. Should the alchemist accidentally spill the cup of Hermes Trismegistus or lose the mercury, the consequences will be dire as the Nadi Chitra (one of the many energy nodes in the body) will surely ignite and the sacred snake will descend. In order to accomplish the great work, it is imperative to submit oneself to the authority of the goddess of justice. Any transgression of the law of balance will lead to the complete collapse of the alchemist's work. It is important to recognize that the construction of the superior existential bodies of the Being is a process rooted in alchemy, and this process must align with the principles of cosmic justice. Failure is inevitable if these principles are disregarded.

Those who fail to purge the inhuman psychic aggregates within themselves cannot achieve unity with divinity. These aggregates, resembling dry Mercury, are present in every human being alongside poisonous Sulfur. The eradication of dry Mercury is essential.

Poisonous Sulfur, residing in the lower animal depths of all living beings, must be removed in order to progress. Additionally, eliminating dry Mercury is essential for any advancement to take place. By removing dry Mercury and toxic Sulfur, it becomes possible to successfully extract gold from Mercury.

By recognizing that the higher spiritual aspects of a person are essentially a combination of Sulfur, Mercury and refined salt, we can grasp the connection between gold and Mercury. The deep connection between gold and Mercury is observable even within mines. Gold atoms are typically secured within Mercury, emphasizing the intimate relationship between these two elements. It is commonly observed that gold is frequently found alongside Mercury.

When the highest existential vessels of humanity are made of pure gold, they undoubtedly act as a shield for the inner metallic spirit that resides in all of us. I am speaking of the Inner Christ, the Interior Magnes of Kabbalah and alchemy, the master. The primary factor of the Great Work is unlocked through the practice of sexual union.

The Latin formula of the Great Arcanum is the following: "Inmisio membri virili in vagina Feminae sine ejeculatium seminis." Refrain from expelling the mercury of the secret philosophy at all costs. Stay away from the bodily orgasm. Remember, this is the essential key to the Great Work.

Undoubtedly, within its profound essence, semen transforms into the mystical mercury of hidden wisdom. Once ignited by the fiery sulphur, it metamorphoses into the ultimate source of power and rejuvenation for mankind, the regenerator of the earthly being. "Odic Light" is the term used by top esoteric writers to describe divine radiations of a sexual nature. As science delves into the astral theory of the human body, it makes sense to utilize terminology from ancient tradition for clarity.

The Od [Hebrew] stands as an indisputable manifestation of brilliant positive active magnetism, under the guidance of the extraordinary power of conscious will. The intelligent faculty known as creative imagination wisely governs the passive magnetic fluid, the Obd [Hebrew]. Within the cosmic amphitheater, the Hebrew term "Aur" stands as the unique illuminating force, representing the genius Lucis.

The famous Caduceus of Mercury, encircled by serpents, embodies a regal depiction of Eros' magnetic charm and harmony. The solar viper on the right symbolizes Od, while the lunar snake on the left represents Obd. At the tip of this enigmatic staff, the globe of Aur shines brightly.

The ancient Alchemists believed that through metaphysical intercourse, the nitrogen and magnesium could undergo incredible transformations within the polarized Astral Light. These intimate changes have a hidden impact on the electrochemical connections within our body's essential components, ultimately leading to a complete structural transformation.

Waldemar says:

"When chemists tell us that all the biocatalysts of an organism appear to be an ordered system of inferior tele-causal factors, which act in accordance with life, in other words in the service of the superior

objectives of the organism, it is not difficult to conclude that the formation of internal emotions, reflections or impulses, depends on the radio-causal factors of the aura. "Let us take a comparative look," says Waldemar, "at the relationship between the living substance of ions and electrons, and we will be considerably nearer to comprehending the aforementioned."

It is abundantly clear that during that extraordinary moment in the garden of pleasures, as the male organ enters deeply into the woman's vagina, a highly unique electrical induction occurs. Without a doubt, the tele-causal elements of the aura experiencing electric impulses present unexpected opportunities. Profound psychological transformation can manifest in the depths of consciousness if we are able to intelligently harness the cosmic opportunity presented to us.

We forego such a remarkable opportunity when our intentions are solely focused on satisfying our senses. Instead of yielding to the insatiable sexual desire, it is more beneficial to engage in prayer; it is inscribed with fiery words in the book of mysteries that intercourse is a form of prayer. During the pinnacle of sexual surrender, amidst intercourse, meditate and pray in order to resist temptation.

The magical power within us lies dormant, coiled three and a half times in the Muladhara chakra, located in the coccygeal bone. By deeply contemplating the connection between the S and the Tao cross, we realize that the awakening of the creative serpent can only be achieved through the practice of Sahaja Maithuna (sexual magic). To unlock the key, one must refrain from spilling the vessel of Hermes (the ens seminis) during the sexual trance. It is crucial to connect the lingam-yoni (phallus-uterus) without releasing the ens seminis, as it holds the dormant power entity of fire.

The transformation of sexual energy into creative power is a well-established principle in Hermetic philosophy. The analysis of the dual nature of cosmic energy in the human body has been a subject of thorough examination in the initiatic schools of Egypt, Mexico, Greece, India, Persia, and more since ancient times.

The remarkable movement of the seminal energy towards the brain is enabled by a specific pair of nerve cords in the form of an eight, gracefully extending to the sides of the spinal column. This brings us to the Caduceus of Mercury, where the wings of the soul are beautifully open. These particular nerve cords cannot be observed with a scalpel. They are more of an ethereal, three-dimensional nature.

Certainly, these are the two witnesses mentioned in Saint John's Apocalypse – "the two olive trees, and the two candlesticks standing before the God of the earth." In the sacred realm of the Vedas, these two nerves are traditionally known as Ida and Pingala, with Ida being linked to the left nostril and Pingala to the right nostril. It is evident that Ida, the first of these two channels, is associated with the moon, while Pingala, the second channel, is of a solar nature.

Ancient customs that seem to appear mysteriously from the depths of time itself tell us that when the solar and lunar atoms of the reproductive system come into contact at the Triveni, a powerful force is awakened through electric induction. This force is none other than the Kundalini, the mystical fire of the Gnostic arhat, which allows us to transcend our animalistic ego and become one with the cosmos.

According to ancient wisdom, it is stated in age-old texts that the lower opening of the spinal cord in ordinary individuals is tightly sealed. However, this seal is broken by the release of seminal vapors, allowing the sacred snake to pass through.

Many mistakenly believe that Kundalini Devi is a mechanical phenomenon. In reality, the fiery serpent can only be aroused through authentic love shared between a husband and wife, and it will never travel up the spinal canal of adulterers.

As Hadit, the luminous winged serpent, awakens and commences its journey up the spinal cord, a peculiar sound resonates, closely resembling the hiss of a viper being taunted with a stick.

Kundalini symbolizes the mystic duality, the Mother-God, referred to as Isis, Mary, or more accurately, Ram-Io, Adonia, Insoberta, Rhea, Cybele, Tonantzin, and so forth; it signifies the transcendental unfolding of each divine Monad within the profound core of our essence.

The holy flame rises based on the virtues of the soul. Sexual alchemy is crucial, yet without purity, spiritual progress remains out of reach.

The Secret of the Golden Flower says:

"Purify the heart, wash the thoughts, stop pleasures, and conserve the seed." "If the thoughts endure, the seed enduring, if the seed endures, the energy endures; if the energy endures, then will the spirit endure. The energy of the kidneys is under the water sign. When the desires are stirred, it runs downward, is directed outward, and creates children. If, in the moment of release, it is not allowed to flow outward, but is led

back by energy the energy of thought so that it penetrates the crucible of the Creative, and refreshes heart and body and nourishes them, that also is the backward-flowing method. Therefore, it is said, The Way of the Elixir of Life depends entirely on the backward-flowing method."

It is essential to redirect the sexual energy upwards and inwards, ensuring that the "cup of Hermes" is never spilled. This reflux technique, also known as return, generates a rotational flow of light that enables the convergence of celestial and terrestrial energies, resulting in the formation of a Golden Flower within the body.

When seminal energy flows outward, it leads to a decrease in spiritual awareness. The individual who triggers the ascent of Kundalini to the head is responsible for awakening the crown chakra, known as the seventh seal of the apocalypse. The Kundalini descends solely when the initiate permits themselves to fall. The initiate falls when they ejaculate the semen.

"The couple must withdraw from the sexual act before reaching the spasm, in order to avoid the spilling of the seminal liquid. Restrained desire will transmute the seminal liquid into creative energy. The sexual energy ascends up to the cerebrum. This is how the cerebrum is seminized; this is how the semen becomes cerebrized. The Maithuna (Sex Magic) is the exercise that permits us to awaken and develop the Kundalini, the igneous serpent of our magical powers. When the Kundalini awakens, it ascends along the medullar canal of the spinal column" – Samael Aun Weor

Bibliography

The Order of The Gnostics by Mr. Moe Bedard – **https://amzn.to/3VRrICB**

The Mystery of Golden Flower by Samel Aun Weor – **https://amzn.to/3VQes1e**

Practical Astrology by Samael Aun Weor – **https://amzn.to/3JcwnHQ**

Treatise of Sexual Alchemy by Samael Aun Weor – **https://amzn.to/43Yjfj5**

5

PROPER BREATHING – THE FIRST STEP TO A LONG HEALTHY LIFE

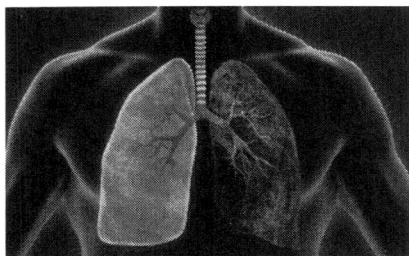

THE WAY YOU BREATHE, controls your life, your look, your energy, your emotions and your resistance to diseases. It controls your very life span". Disease runs in families because bad habits run in families. To be healthy is to be a rebel. It is the ultimate rebellion in a diseased, sick and dysfunctional society. Most people would think that to be healthy it is important to eat healthy.

There is more to health than just what you eat. Being healthy is when you take care of your physical, mental, emotional, and spiritual body. You can go to the gym, drink water, take vitamins all you want but if your head and heart are disturbed with muddy thoughts, you will still be unhealthy.

You are much more than just your physical body. In this first part we will focus on physical health.

Breathing is the most underrated health necessity. Humans take it for granted. I am talking about deep breathing and not shallow irregular breathing that most humans are accustomed to. There are at least two types of breathing: 1- **Cleansing** (exhalation) 2- **Energizing** (inhalation).

Energizing breath collects and stores vital energy and focuses more on inhalation. Cleansing breath detoxifies the body and stresses exhalation. The act of breathing not only extracts Chi/chee (ethericbasic substance that all living things are made of) from air, but it also drives and distributes Chi through the body's invisible network of energy channels, called meridians. In Asia breathing is regarded as a science.

China has Nei-Gong/Tai-Chi, India has pranayama. The western world lacks a specific term for breath control. Western physicians fail to innerstand how atmospheric energy serves as a vital nutrient for human health.

The essential element in air that carries the vital charge of Chi (life-force energy), is neither oxygen nor nitrogen but rather the negative ion, a tiny, highly active molecular fragment that carries a negative electrical charge equivalent to that of one electron.

In nature air is naturally ionized by the action of shortwave electromagnetic radiation from the sun and by the other cosmic rays, which bombard air molecules and impart vital energy to the fragments. Breathing therapy is an established homeopathic medical procedure in Chinese tradition. And the western world slowly but surely is picking up on it.

Deep breathing massages internal organs and glands, purges tissues of toxins, purifies the bloodstream, stimulates hormone secretions, and enhances resistance and immunity. Dr. Sun Ssu-mo wrote about therapeutic deep breathing in Precious Recipes:

When correct breathing is practiced, the myriad ailments will not occur. When breathing is depressed or strained, all sorts of diseases will arise. Those who wish to nurture their lives must first learn the correct methods of controlling breath and balancing energy. These breathing methods can cure all ailments great and small.

The majority of humans take short and shallow breaths into the upper chest area. They receive a small amount of their lung's air capacity. Unfortunately, short, and shallow breaths also stimulate the sympathetic nervous system, the fight or flight response to stress.

Because of this, cortisol the stress hormone is released into the bloodstream.

This taxes our adrenal glands, and it negatively impacts the whole body. If this is your unconscious/automatic breathing, then you need to retrain yourself to naturally breathe in a deep and relaxed way. To breathe is to live, to not breathe is to die. Do you know there is a quick pause between breaths? You can think of that as little death.

To not breathe is to die, in this case it is about not breathing deeply. Your body is designed to breathe deeply with the diaphragm. Not using the diaphragm means that your body is not functioning the way it is supposed to. Try to drive a car without having changed the oil when it is required to or if you drive a car as soon as you turn it on without waiting for it to warm up. What do you think will happen?

At the beginning you might not see a difference but if you continue to do this, then the car will start to break down. Now, do you see what can happen if you don't feed the body with prana/Chi (life force energy) the way it is supposed to? It will break down.

CELLUAR RESPIRATION

In his book *The Illuminated Breath*, Dylan Werner stated that we breathe primarily for the purpose of taking in oxygen through inhalation and eliminating waste gases through exhalation. Both sides of the breath cycle support cellular respiration – the process cells undergo to create energy. The complicated chemistry behind this process can be difficult to understand, but the basic idea is simple.

The food we eat is broken down through digestion to make fuel for our cells .[*the cleaner the food (raw food) the cleaner the fuel for our cells*]. The primary fuel is glucose. Glucose and oxygen combine inside little organelles in the cells called mitochondria. The mitochondria then convert glucose and oxygen to carbon dioxide, water, and energy.

The energy comes in the form of adenosine triphosphate, or ATP, which the body is able to use for fuel. And this gives the lungs their main job, which is to bring in oxygen to facilitate cellular respiration and breathe out carbon dioxide and water. Typically, we don't think we are expelling water, but if you exhale into your hand, you can feel the humidity.

A more tangible illustration of this phenomenon involves fogging up a cold piece of glass by breathing on it. The fog is nothing more than water and heat from your breath. Breathing also plays a considerable role in regulating the pH levels of our blood.

Human Blood pH Level

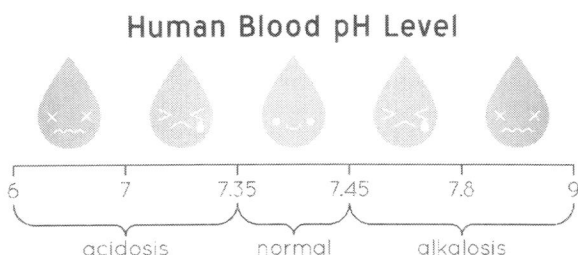

Normal blood pH is 7.4, but it varies from 7.35 to 7.45. *As we breathe faster, our pH levels rise, and we become more alkaline. As we slow the breath down, our pH levels drop, and we become more acidic.* Our bodies continuously monitor and regulate our blood pH by varying the rate and depth of our breathing as needed.

If we're at rest, our breath is slow and shallow, but if we go for a run, we breathe faster and deeper. That rapid breathing reflects the body's increase in both energy use and production of carbon dioxide, which lowers blood pH (making it more acidic). So, to regulate that, we need to exhale all that extra carbon dioxide.

THE CARBONIC-BICARBONATE BUFFER SYSTEM

Through its normal metabolic process, the body releases hydrogen ions (H+), which make the blood more acidic. If there are too many hydrogen ions in the blood, the body combines them with bicarbonate (HCO_3 -) to form carbonic acid (H_2CO_3). It is able to break down the carbonic acid into carbon dioxide (CO_2) and water (H_2O), which are then exhaled, resulting in a rise in alkalinity.

But if we become too alkaline, carbon dioxide combines the water in the blood to make carbonic acid, and the blood becomes more acidic to neutralize the excessive alkalinity. Breathing is controlled by our autonomic nervous system and our central nervous system, meaning that it is generally an involuntary process that we can override to a certain extent.

Therefore, we can voluntarily hyperventilate and raise our blood pH levels until we feel dizzy and light-headed, have tingling sensations in the face and body, and have muscle spasms in the hands and feet. If we are breathing hard and fast for a long time, we might eventually pass out.

We can also try to hold our breath for a long time until our diaphragm starts to spasm and we experience an intense sensation known as air hunger. If we are trained and disciplined, we might be able to fight the urge to breathe until we pass out. Usually, though, the autonomic nervous system takes control before we lose consciousness and restores our natural breathing.

In most cases, we don't want to bring ourselves to such extremes willingly, but our ability to consciously change the rate, rhythm, and depth of the breath gives us the power to use the breath as an effective too for bettering our health, emotional state, and well-being.

We think we need to breathe more to get more oxygen into our cells, but it is actually carbon dioxide that plays an essential role in making this exchange happen. Also, we can't get more oxygen into our cells just by taking in more air. The main reason is that our blood is already fully saturated with oxygen.

Normal blood oxygen saturation for a healthy person is between 95 and 99 percent; this means that the hemoglobin on the red blood cells is already carrying as much oxygen as it can handle.

Trying to squeeze in more oxygen doesn't result in any improvement, just as trying to squeeze one or two more passengers into a packed subway car wouldn't result in any improvement to the mode of transportation or the harmony of those being transported.

(A common myth is that if we breathe more, we get more oxygen. Normal blood oxygen saturation for a healthy person is between 95 and 99 percent. The circulatory system acts like a series of subway lines, and our oxygen-carrying red blood cells are like subway cars, delivering oxygen to the body. If the cars are full, trying to cram in more people isn't going to help. Instead, we need to increase the number of cars (red blood cells) and the efficiency of getting people on and off the train.)

CARBON DIOXIDE AND THE BOHR EFFECT

Why do we feel dizzy when we breathe too fast? To answer this question, we need to understand the role of carbon dioxide. First, carbon dioxide plays a significant role in every breath we take. It's a common misconception that we breathe because we are running low on oxygen.

We are stimulated to breathe based on how much carbon dioxide is in our blood. (The exception is people who have chronic respiratory problems, such as emphysema or chronic obstructive pulmonary disease, or COPD, who live with abnormally high levels of carbon dioxide and breathe based on low oxygen).

As we hold our breath, chemoreceptors sense the decrease in pH (more acidic) and the increase in carbon dioxide; this stimulates us to take the next breath. The higher the carbon dioxide levels, the stronger the desire is to breathe.

This urge is why it gets harder and harder to hold our breath for a long time. Generally, when we experience that strong urge to breathe, we still have plenty of oxygen in our blood.

Dylan states, when he measures his blood oxygen levels while holding his breath, he don't see a drop in oxygen saturation until around three minutes of retention, and this is long after he has an urge to breathe.

The time it takes for S_PO_2 (peripheral capillary oxygen saturation) levels to drop varies from person to person and depends on a variety of factors, the main one being how many red blood cells are in the body.

As we breath, the hemoglobin in the red blood cells bind to oxygen as it passes through the lungs, creating oxyhemoglobin. The red blood cells then go out to the body to supply our cells with oxygen.

The only problem is that for the red blood cells to release oxygen, oxyhemoglobin needs carbon dioxide to increase blood acidity to facilitate the cellular exchange. This physiological event is called the Bohr effect, named after Nobel Prize – winning Danish physician Christian Bohr.

The Bohr effect states, "Hemoglobin's oxygen binding affinity is inversely related both to acidity and to the concentration of carbon dioxide."

Hemoglobin is an iron-rich oxygen-carrying protein inside red blood cells. There are about 270 million hemoglobin molecules per red blood cell, and each hemoglobin molecule can carry oxygen molecules.

That means each red blood cell can hold over a billion oxygen molecules. As carbon dioxide levels rise due to cellular respiration, blood pH becomes more acidic, and the bond between the oxygen and hemoglobin is loosened so that oxygen can be released into the cells.

If carbon dioxide levels are low and blood pH is high, the red blood cells can't release oxygen to the cells. The body is the ultimate "use it or lose it" system. Whatever we do, our bodies work to support us. If we run, our bodies will work in a way to help us become better at running.

Our leg muscles will get stronger, our tendons will become more bouncy and elastic, and our endurance will increase. If we practice sitting on the couch, our bodies are going to get really good at sitting on the couch.

The body's main concern is survival, and our survival is dependent on having the energy to fuel the body as well as store reserves to get more energy when fuel starts to run low.

Muscles take a lot of energy, which is why our muscles atrophy when we stop exercising. Fat is the body's way to store energy, which is why it stores an excess it receives as adipose tissue. Every second, approximately 2 to 2.5 million of our red blood cells die, and about the same number are created in our bone marrow to replace them. Those red blood cells will live for three to four months before they are replaced with new ones based on the body's current demands.

"Current demands" are important to understand. Our bodies respond to what we've been doing; it doesn't know what we are going to need to do. If we are breathing too much, our carbon dioxide levels stay low, and the red blood cells can't release oxygen. As a result, the body thinks it has too many red blood cells, so it doesn't replace them when they die. We are then left with the bare minimum number of red blood cells we need to survive. In this state, if we decided to go for a run, we would become winded rather quickly.

Chronic over-breathers also can't hold their breath very long. When they do, their S_PO_2 levels drop quickly because they don't have extra red blood cells circulating to meet the new demand.

So carbon dioxide stimulates us to breathe and allows oxygen to be released from the red blood cells so that it can be used by muscles, organs, and every other cell in the body. Carbon dioxide also opens our airways, which is called bronchodilation, so we can breathe better.

It expands our blood vessels, called vasodilation, which lowers blood pressure and allows the blood to perfuse our extremities with less effort by the heart. The opposite happens when carbon dioxide levels are low (a state known as hypocapnia).

Our airways get smaller and our blood vessels going to the brain constrict. In turn, the brain receives significantly less blood and oxygen, which is why we feel light-headed and dizzy when we hyperventilate. This familiar response is not from too much oxygen; it's from too little.

Bringing more oxygen into the brain makes us feel clear, aware, and focused. Increasing carbon dioxide levels through breathing less offers many amazing benefits, which is why so many of the practices we will post on the breath in our weekly blog articles (at https://theserpentsway.com/) are focused on holding the breath, slowing components of the breath, or simply creating good habits of breathing less.

The majority of people who over-breathe are not aware that they do it. When you go out in public, notice how many people are breathing through their mouths. Anyone who is mouth breathing is over-breathing. The nose creates about 50 percent more airflow restriction than the mouth.

In other words, if we are breathing through our mouths, we are breathing twice as much as we should, and it's a downward spiral from there. Mouth breathing leads to lower levels of carbon dioxide, which means the red blood cells can't release oxygen into our tissues, and our cells aren't adequately perfused.

The red blood cells return to the lungs still carrying their full oxygen load. The body recognizes this as a waste of energy, and since making new red blood cells takes energy, it doesn't replace those returning cells because it doesn't think it needs to.

This means less oxygen carrying hemoglobin, which means anytime we do anything, we'll need to breathe faster and deeper, which again lowers carbon dioxide level. And, unfortunately, this cycle continues.

THE UPPER RESPIRATORY SYSTEM

The mouth is made for talking, eating and drinking, and the nose is designed for breathing. There are breathing exercises that involve inhaling through the mouth and exercises where you purposefully exhale as much carbon dioxide as possible.

Otherwise, nasal breathing is the proper way to breathe. Respiration starts with the nose. Generally, one nostril is restricted, while the other is mostly clear. About every four hours, the inside of nostril becomes swollen, and the other opens up.

This phenomenon is called the nasal cycle, and about 80 percent of people experience this switching of one nostril or the other being closed to some degree. The nasal cycle works to alternate the workload of breathing so that the mucous membranes inside the nose don't dry out, and it also helps improve our sense of smell by allowing air to enter both fast and slowly through the clear and partially restricted nostrils.

Beyond smelling and down-regulating air intake, the nose has many other functions. It is responsible for warming, humidifying, and filtering the air we breathe in, moving air along the respiratory mucosa inside the nasal cavity.

The lungs require warm moist air, regardless of how cold it might be outside or how high the air-conditioning is cranked. But one of the most amazing functions of the nose is its ability to increase levels of nitric oxide through inspiration, which is something we don't get from mouth breathing.

THE SIGNIFICANCE OF NITRIC OXIDE

Nitric Oxide is a signaling molecule that is made in the lining of the blood vessels, in the nasal cavity, and in the paranasal sinus. As we inhale through the nose, nitric oxide is carried into our lungs and through the rest of the body. Nitric oxide has a long list of health benefits:

(1) *It works alongside carbon dioxide to assist with oxygen binding and to release and increase cellular oxygen uptake by 10 to 20 percent.*

(2) *It is a smooth muscle relaxer and vasodilator, working to regulate and lower blood pressure and improve circulation and control vascular tone.*

(3) *It increases the health and elasticity of blood vessels, lowers cholesterol, and decreases plaque buildup, which has a significant impact on cardiovascular health.*

People with low levels of nitric oxide are more likely to have cardiac problems such as high blood pressure and heart attacks, as well as an increased risk of stroke. As we get older, nitric oxide production naturally decreases, so working to increase nitric oxide levels through proper breathing as well as diet is vital for our overall health.

Along with general cardiovascular health, nitric oxide is one of the miracle molecules for increasing strength and fitness and decreasing recovery time. Because it's a vasodilator, having higher levels of nitric oxide means that more blood and oxygen can perfuse our muscles; increased circulation also helps reduce lactic acid buildup, delayed-onset muscle soreness (DOMS), and fatigue.

Nitric oxide promotes cell proliferation, which is the growth and reproduction of cells. It also helps increase oxygen delivery the mitochondria, which gives us much more energy to be active. Nitric oxide works to decrease inflammation, increase the production of antioxidants, and improves immune system function. In addition to these physical benefits, nitric oxide is a powerful neurotransmitter that aids in the rapid communication between brain cells, which increases learning capacity, concentration, and memory.

Because nitric oxide isn't produced during mouth breathing, mouth breathers experience a massive decrease in levels of nitric oxide. Multiple studies have shown that children who mouth breathe are more likely to have learning disabilities than children who nasal breathe. Ultimately, the importance of both nitric oxide and nasal breathing with regard to learning is incontrovertible.

When we breathe in slowly through the nose, we take in more nitric oxide than when we breathe fast. Slow nasal breathing has a profound calming and relaxing effect, with impacts on the brain that are similar to those of dopamine and serotonin, two other types of neurotransmitters.

Nitric oxide also works to regulate the sympathetic nervous system, which governs our cardiovascular system and our fight-or-flight response, as you'll learn about later. Its ability to help control our reaction to perceived danger lessens the effect we feel when we are afraid, stressed, or nervous.

This is why our bodies and minds are best served by taking slow, calm breaths when we find ourselves in stressful or scary situations. Because nitric oxide both is a vasodilator and positively influences the autonomic nervous system, it helps increase libido and sexual function.

Sex drive and sexual function are highly emotionally based. Our automatic nervous system has a significant impact on sexual function in both men and women. Stress is the leading cause of sexual and erectile dysfunction, because when we are stressed, the sympathetic nervous system overrides the parasympathetic nervous system. There needs to be sufficient parasympathetic tone for a man to have an erection and for a woman to produce vaginal lubrication. Nitric oxide helps calm the mind, alleviate stress, and reestablish healthy function of the parasympathetic nervous system.

The other chief function of nitric oxide, vasodilation, acts to increase blood flow to the genitalia. Men get a harder erection, and women get more blood flow to the clitoris, creating more pressure, more sensitivity, and more intense orgasms.

Drugs like Viagra and Cialis work by enhancing nitric oxide-mediated vasodilation in the erectile tissues, and studies have shown that they are effective in both men and women.

THE LUNGS

Returning to the anatomy of the upper respiratory system as we descend from the mouth and nose, we arrive at the trachea, or windpipe. The trachea is a rigid tube held open by C-shaped rings made of hard cartilage.

This rigidity is essential; without it, the trachea would collapse every time we took a breath. The trachea divides into two bronchi, which split into the right and left lungs. The bronchi continue to divide into bronchioles, and this division happens twenty-five more times, creating an airway system that looks similar to the roots of a tree.

The bronchioles end in ductlike structures called alveoli, where the majority of gas exchange takes place. Men's lungs hold about 6 liters of air, while the average woman's lungs hold about 4,5 liters. Women's lungs are usually 20 to 25 percent smaller than men's.

These values are general, and different textbooks might have different numbers, so please don't get caught up on these values; your lung volume might be completely different.

Total lung capacity also depends on a person's age, height, history of smoking, athletic training/conditioning habits, and numerous other factors. Despite these general numbers, we have the ability to change our vital lung capacity – in other words, how much air we can inhale and how deeply we can exhale.

Whether it is possible to stretch lung tissue is a point of contention among researchers, but either way, we can stretch the thoracic cavity that contains the lungs. Think about blowing up a balloon inside a glass jar. The size of the balloon is limited to the size of the jar.

Our chest and lungs share a similar relationship. World-record-holding freediver Stig Severinsen's lungs can hold 14 liters, which he attributes to the breathing exercises he does to increase his ability to hold his breath for extended periods.

The amount of air we displace during normal breathing, or the unconscious breathing we do while at rest, is called tidal volume, and it's usually about one-tenth of total lung capacity, or around 0,5 liter/500 milliliters (mL), which is the average for both men and women. (Men's tidal volume is typically between 550 and 650 mL; for women, it's 450 to 550 mL.)

When breathing normally, we breathe from the middle range of our lungs. From the upper limit of our tidal volume to our maximum inhalation is called the inspiratory reserve volume, and this about 3 liters (3000 mL).

From the lower limit of our tidal volume, where the diaphragm is relaxed, to the maximum forced exhalation is called the expiratory reserve volume, which is about 1,5 liters (1500mL).

Even after we exhale as much as we can, we still have about 1 liter (1000mL) of air left in our lungs; this is called the residual volume. The residual volume keeps the alveolar sacs from collapsing and keeps enough air in the lungs so that the oxygen exchange can happen even after we exhale or while we hold our breath after exhaling.

When we start at the bottom limit of our maximum exhalation and inhale until we reach the top limit of our maximum inhalation, that's called vital lung capacity. Our vital capacity is essentially the total amount of air we can forcefully move in one breath.

Vital capacity significantly impacts health. Having a low capacity puts us at a higher risk of respiratory disease, and it's directly related to the mortality rate. Our vital capacity decreases with age, but increasing vital capacity has been shown to help slow the aging process.

O_2 MAX

Another marker to gauge fitness, health, and risk of mortality is VO_2 max, which stands for volume oxygen maximum. VO_2 max is the maximum amount of oxygen that the body can intake and deliver to the muscles during maximum effort.

The higher our VO_2 max, the better our cardiorespiratory fitness. Having a higher VO_2 max makes us better at activities like running, swimming, and biking, and it is an accurate marker for health and mortality.

While most cardio exercises focus on increasing the heart rate, we can improve our VO_2 max just through breathing exercises and essentially become better at cardio without doing traditional cardio exercises.

Werner is not suggesting that you give up cardio exercise and focus only on breathing, but if you also work on the respiratory side of cardiorespiratory fitness, you will increase your endurance, fitness level, and overall health and well-being.

THE MUSCLES OF RESPIRATION

The diaphragm, a thin, dome-shaped muscle that separates the thoracic or chest cavity from the abdominal cavity, is the primary muscle of inhalation and exhalation. The basic mechanics of breathing involve nothing more than simple pressure differentials.

To inhale, we reduce the pressure inside our body so that it is less than the atmospheric pressure. The air outside our body rushes into our lungs to equalize these pressures.

To exhale, the diaphragm relaxes and returns to its dome shape, which makes the thoracic cavity smaller, increasing the internal pressure and forcing the air out.

We find it harder to breathe when we climb in the mountains because the atmospheric pressure is lower at higher altitudes, so we have to work harder to lower our internal pressure.

The diaphragm lowers internal pressure by pulling or flattening out and expanding the space inside the chest. Through normal tidal volume breathing, the diaphragm does almost all the work, and exhalation is completely passive.

The diaphragm relaxes, and the natural tension in the thoracic cavity plus the outside atmospheric pressure aids in an effortless exhale. We breathe more than our normal tidal volume; we need to recruit our accessory breathing muscles.

Increasing the effort to breathe is called forced inhalation or exhalation because inhaling and exhaling requires more force than normal.

While the diaphragm still does the majority of the work for inhalation, the external intercostals, serratus anterior, sternocleidomastoid muscle, and scalene muscles assist in lifting the ribs and further expands the chest. *The more we open and expand the chest, the lower our inner pressure becomes, and therefore the deeper inhalation.*

For forced exhalation, we need to increase the inner pressure in our chest. The diaphragm can aid in exhalation only until it returns to its relaxed dome shape. The intercostal muscles and abdominal muscles do most of the work by pulling the ribs down and making the chest cavity smaller.

Really, the abdominis rectus (our six-pack muscles) are the main muscles working. Many people breathe poorly and insufficiently due to constant engagement of the abdominal muscles, which are our muscles of exhalation.

The main reason is that people don't want to let their bellies hang out. Even beyond forced respiration, walking around with our core muscles continuously engaged limits our ability to breathe fully and effortlessly.

The core muscles hold the bottom ribs down and belly in, which impedes the diaphragm, in turn forcing the accessory inhale – centric muscles to work harder in order to lift the upper chest and collarbones because we can't expand the bottom ribs or breathe down into the abdominal region.

This is known as chest breathing, and it is a tremendous waste of energy, resulting in insufficient shallow breathing. Breathing with the core consistently engaged can also move us into a chronic state of tension and stress that negatively impacts the health and balance of our autonomic nervous system.

You might have heard of diaphragmatic breathing or belly breathing, which refers to breathing with a relaxed core, allowing the stomach to expand. It's a common misconception that when we belly breathe, we are using only our diaphragm, and when we chest breathe, we are using only our accessory chest muscles.

Chest breathing doesn't mean that the diaphragm is not functioning. The diaphragm is working in every type of breathing we do.

If you've ever had the wind knocked out of you, either from falling flat on your back or being hit in the stomach or solar plexus, you've experienced a temporary paralysis of the diaphragm, and it can feel like you can't breathe without using your diaphragm.

"Breath is the bridge which connects life to consciousness, which unties your body to your thoughts. Whenever your mind becomes scattered, use your breath as the means to take hold of your mind again" – Thich Nhat Hanh

CLINICAL VALUES VS BASELINE VALUES

Werner states, there is always going to be high variability between what medical textbooks say our normal vital signs should be and the actual numbers in healthy and unhealthy people, for example, a regular pulse rate should be between 60 and 100 beats per minute (bpm).

Below 60 bpm is considered bradycardia, or too slow to circulate the blood and deliver oxygen to the cells adequately. Most athletes and healthy people have a lower-than-average resting heart rate.

Clinical standards are supposed to be based on the average person. Unfortunately, with the majority of Americans being overweight or obese and sedentary, normal standards don't represent the health-conscious, active population.

Clinical baselines give us a starting point, but knowing your baseline vitals and how changes in your heart rate, respiratory rate, blood pressure, and other baselines make you feel is better than any set of numbers you will find in a book.

However, if your pulse rate, breathing rate, or blood pressure is higher than the clinical average, then it should raise significant concern. I've never met a healthy person whose resting heart rate was over 100 bpm.

Things like health and wellness, which should be our responsibility, are not. Instead, we pass our health to other people, like doctors, to "fix". Usually, the fixes do not actually heal us.

We mask problems, using pharmaceutical interventions to manipulate conditions such as hypertension (high blood pressure) and tachycardia (rapid heart rate) into "normal" limits, but we never address the real problems, which are easily fixed or prevented by eating better, breathing better, and moving more.

Consider the "normal" clinical numbers as tools, not goals. Your goals should be based on where you are now and working to improve upon that. The clinical values for a normal breathing rate are twelve to twenty breaths per minute, although the upper limit of twenty breaths per minute is probably over-breathing for a healthy person.

Generally, people who are overweight and have a larger body mass have faster and more labored breathing. Most fit, healthy people, especially those with good breathing habits, like nasal breathing with a relaxed belly, breathe between ten and sixteen times per minute.

Measuring our breathing rate can be tricky, because as soon as we start thinking about it, we change the way we breathe. Werner states that when he would take a patient's vital signs, he would pretend to take their pulse while counting the rise and fall of their chest so that he could get an accurate respiration rate.

Again, we move about 500 mL of air during one breath cycle. If we are taking ten breaths per minute, that is the equivalent of breathing 5 liters of air per minute.

If our total lung capacity is 6 liters, then our vital capacity, or how much air we can move in one full breath, is around 5 liters, with 1 liter remaining as our residual volume.

So why is it important to know how much air we're breathing? I've mentioned some of the disadvantages of over-breathing, but we haven't looked at the many advantages that come from breathing less.

"There is one way of breathing that is shameful and constricted. Then there's another way; a breath of love that takes you all the way to infinity" – Rumi

THE BENEFITS OF UNDER-BREATHING

Werner states that almost all health professionals preach the value of being more alkaline. Drinking alkaline water and eating a more alkaline diet have been shown to have many health benefits, like lowering inflammation, chronic pain, and the risk of illness and disease.

Changing the pH of the blood for any length of time is difficult because of the body's amazing buffering system. Our bodies regulate our blood to remain around a constant pH of 7.4. A sustained change in blood pH is usually the result of a more serious health problem.

Although we can mildly change the pH quickly just by breathing fast or slowly, it returns to baseline almost immediately after we resume normal breathing. But the pH of the rest of our bodies' fluids varies a lot more and is significantly affected by the foods we eat.

The body is also always looking for homeostasis, which is a state of physiological equilibrium. Over-breathing temporarily increases blood pH and makes us more alkaline.

It also makes us feel hungrier and crave acid-forming foods, like sugars, fats, complex carbohydrates, and processed foods. Generally, over-breathing makes us want the foods that we should limit.

The next time you do something that causes you to breathe fast, like sprinting or burpees, notice how hungry you feel afterward and which types of foods you crave.

Werner notices that when he teaches all day, he usually is starving later. It's hard to talk for longer periods without over-breathing. Under-breathing (aka hypoventilation) has the opposite effect.

When we breathe less, our blood pH decreases and we become more acidic, which has the effect of suppressing appetite and leads to cravings for more alkaline-forming foods, like fruits and vegetables.

HIGH-ALTITUDE TRAINING EFFECTS FROM BREATHING EXERCISES

Werner stated that his high school was 5,600 feet (1,700 meters) above sea level. Although it was a small school, his wrestling team usually dominated the much larger schools.

When teams from other schools would come up the mountain to compete against his school, most of his opponents would run out of breath and struggle to keep up because they weren't used to the thinner air.

When he wrestled at schools that were closer to sea level, he felt like he had so much more energy and endurance. Training at high elevation boosted his team's red blood cell count, so they had more oxygen-carrying hemoglobin to supply their muscles, which increased his team's cardio fitness (VO2 max) and endurance.

They would often win because the other teams were too tired to keep up. What gave them the advantage over other schools is known as high-altitude training, although most people who do high-altitude training train at much higher elevations, and some endurance athletes even train at elevations higher than 8,000 feet (2,400 meters).

Because the air is thinner at higher altitudes, it is harder for the body to deliver oxygen to the cells than it is at sea level, so the body makes more red blood cells to keep up with metabolic demands.

Many Olympic training centers are located at high elevation to give athletes an advantage. Lance Armstrong is known as one of the greatest cyclists ever, and he is the only person to have won the Tour de France seven times. However, he was stripped of all his victories after being accused of blood doping.

Blood doping involves artificially increasing the number of red blood cells in the bloodstream to boost athletic performance, and some of the methods used can be very dangerous. Most sports have deemed blood doping illegal.

Whether we are training at high altitude or (preferably not) blood doping, having more oxygen-carrying red blood cells increases our athletic performance. As discussed earlier, the body works off of demand.

Whatever the body needs, it generates more of; if there is an excess or a lack of need, the body makes less. Chronic over-breathing results in fewer red blood cells, but under-breathing produces more.

Breathing less, particularly long breath-holds and breath retention while performing strenuous activities, can simulate high-altitude training and has the same physiological effect.

Creating an oxygen-deficient environment and increasing carbon dioxide prompts the body to make more red blood cells to meet our needs, which results in increased cardiorespiratory fitness and endurance levels.

Have you ever been running and felt a "second wind"— a boost of energy and endurance? The spleen filters the blood, recycles old red blood cells, and holds a significant reserve of red blood cells in case of a sudden drop in blood pressure or inadequate circulation.

If we are engaged in strenuous activity, the spleen contracts and releases a large number of red blood cells into our system, resulting in that second wind.

Breath retention exercises can also be used to stimulate splenic contraction. When we do multiple rounds of long breath-holds, the spleen releases more and more red blood cells into circulation, which is why holding the breath usually gets easier the more rounds we do.

We can also get this extra boost of red blood cells before doing an activity for which we are going to want extra endurance by practicing several rounds of breath retention first so that we don't have to wait for the second wind.

Breathing less also decreases pain perception, improves mood, stabilizes emotions, brings about deep states of relaxation, and helps us feel more at peace.

>*"Improper breathing is a common cause of ill health" – Dr. Andrew Well*

OVER-BREATHING IN YOGA

Werner who is a renowned international yoga instructor, stated that he initially came to understand the breath and breathing practices through yoga. The ironic thing he stated is that it took him years of practicing and studying the breath to realize how much he was over-breathing in yoga.

He started with power yoga, which, as the name suggests, is a very physical practice. Much like ashtanga vinyasa, another prevalent form of yoga, it has a strong focus on a loud and forceful kind of breath called ujjayi pranayama.

He's not implying that ujjayi breathing is always loud and forceful, but all the power yoga teachers from whom he learned taught it this way. Ujjayi is an audible breath, where the practitioner constricts their throat the way they would if they were trying to whisper with their mouth closed.

This constriction of the glottis creates a hissing sound as the practitioner inhales and exhales through the nose. When this breath is practiced in power yoga, ashtanga vinyasa, and many other strong forms of yoga, the practitioner also needs to activate all the accessory breathing muscles, like the core and intercostals, to make the breath audible.

Most teachers encourage making the breath as loud as possible, which increases the force and energy exertion. The breath is also much deeper and fuller than it would normally be at rest, and although it is slow, the natural pauses at the top and bottom of the breath are usually shortened or skipped.

Ujjayi is an excellent breath for building heat in the body and focusing the mind on the breath. Still, it can be a massive waste of energy and a form of unnecessary over-breathing if not used appropriately, especially if we are practicing yoga for ninety minutes or longer in mostly static postures.

When the yoga practice is physically intense, our increased metabolic rate can make up for the excess carbon dioxide that we are losing from the increased breathing. But breathing more than needed comes with a physiological price.

He's not suggesting you stop your ujjayi breath practice during yoga; he just wants to bring awareness to what is happening physiologically and offer ways to modify the practice to serve you better and help clarify your intention.

Ujjayi is a powerful tool when used right! Even if you are not doing ujjayi, are you aware of the intensity of your breath, and are you breathing more than you need to? Could you breathe less?

If we do ujjayi breath while holding a triangle pose and breathe very slowly at ten times per minute, but also breathe very deeply at 3 liters per breath (which isn't a full breath, but about two-thirds of our vital capacity), we are breathing 30 liters of air per minute.

With our normal breath, we breathe 5 liters per minute; however, our deep ujjayi breath delivers six times as much air as we would need to breathe while holding this pose! We all need to breathe deeper and faster as we exercise.

This doesn't mean we are over-breathing; it means we are breathing to meet our bodies' increased metabolic demand. Adverse or harmful effects can occur when we continuously breathe more than is needed. We want to work on breathing less in almost everything we do.

Even if we engaged in a practice that centers on breathing faster, we balance the increased pace with breath-holds so that overall, we are breathing less. We can compare over-breathing to over-eating.

If we chronically over-eat, we become accustomed to the increased caloric intake, even though our bodies don't need more food. Too much food means that we can become overweight or obese, and our health will decline.

When we go on a diet, our bodies initially feel like they're starving from the lack of unnecessary calories that they were used to getting. After continuously eating less, the body eventually adjusts to the new diet, and the cravings to over-eat diminish, ultimately leading to weight loss and improved health.

Similarly, when we start breathing less, initially our bodies feel like it's not getting enough air because it's used to the excess oxygen it receives from over-breathing.

In the beginning, the body also has fewer red blood cells to support breathing less, as well as a lower tolerance to carbon dioxide. Just like beginning a diet, training the body to accept a new norm takes time. Also like a diet, it is easy to relapse into old habits. Learning to breathe less takes time and consistency.

LEARNING TO BREATHE LESS

To breathe less Werner states, we need to understand how much air we are breathing in one minute while at rest and during exercise. Once we know our baseline, we can work on reducing those numbers.

There are several ways to do this, and all of them involve changing either the depth of each breath (not breathing as deeply) or the number of breaths taken in a minute. We start by figuring out our average respiration rate and tidal volume.

Let's stick with the example of breathing 500 mL of air per breath at ten breaths per minute, or 5 liters per minute. To breathe less, we need to breathe slower than ten breaths per minute.

If we take one full breath from empty lungs, this would also be 5 liters, and we would need to hold this breath for one minute to meet our baseline of 5 liters per minute. To breathe less, we would need to hold our breath longer than one minute.

Ultimately, trying to calculate what is less than normal can be difficult. The results are often inaccurate because measuring how much you're breathing requires a spirometer, a tool used by respiratory therapists.

Let's move away from numbers being the goal, but keep in mind what your average feels like. Since the advantages of breathing less really comes from increasing carbon dioxide levels, let's focus on this goal.

Sensation and stimulation to breathe comes from increased carbon dioxide in the blood, called hypercapnia. We will use our drive to breathe to understand how much we are breathing.

At rest, we usually don't notice the need to take a breath; the body breathes automatically. But if we hold our breath for a few moments, we will quickly feel the need to breathe, a sensation known as breath hunger.

Building up our carbon dioxide levels and increasing our tolerance to carbon dioxide, which decreases the feeling of breath hunger, is the best way to start training to breathe less.

People who chronically over-breathe develop a lower tolerance to carbon dioxide, so they are driven to breathe much faster than needed. Increasing carbon dioxide tolerance through practicing breath retention creates a new baseline that restores normal respiratory rates.

If you are an over-breather, a mouth breather, a chest breather, or all three, then establishing good breathing habits is your number one priority. Luckily, it is easy to change the way you breathe by creating some new patterns and breaking some old ones.

It just takes a little time, awareness, and consistency. Breathing naturally and correctly is simple and takes only a minute to learn, but implementing the habit can take weeks or months. Even while retraining how to breathe correctly, you can work on breathing less.

"It was long ago realized that understanding and working with our breathing was the most effective way to build a bridge between the physical and energetic realms" – Damo Mitchell

POSTURE AND THE BREATH

Take a breath. If you feel that you are growing taller or your shoulders and collarbones are lifting, then you are likely chest breathing. A natural breath shouldn't be forced states Werner; it should be effortless, with little or no noticeable assistance from the accessory breathing muscles, like the intercostals or neck muscles.

Even if you take a deep breath, your shoulders and collarbones shouldn't rise; instead, you should feel your rib cage expand outward. Healthy and effective breathing starts with good posture.

One reason poor posture is so bad for us is that it significantly impairs the diaphragm's ability to function properly. Think of a drum head (the part you strike to make noise).

It sounds best when it is pulled uniformly taut. If you squeeze the opening of the drum, then you will warp the drum head, and the drumming will sound awful.

The diaphragm is similar; it works best when it is equally taut, as it naturally is when we have good posture. When we slouch forward and roll our shoulders in, the chest compresses and the sternum and rib cage have trouble expanding.

The diaphragm isn't able to contract properly and pull down to expand our chest as we inhale. Poor posture leads to compensatory breathing patterns, like lifting the shoulders and collarbones, which can lead to chronic back pain.

These types of compensatory breathing patterns also stimulate the nervous system's stress responses that can create feelings of anxiety and depression. For proper posture, whether sitting or standing, the spine should maintain its natural curve.

The lower lumbar spine should have a mild lordotic or inward-curving shape. The upper thoracic spine should have a mild kyphotic or outward-curving shape, and the neck should have a natural lordotic curve where the head is not extending forward.

The shoulders should be slightly forward in a neutral position and not pulled back like a soldier when standing at attention. The pelvis should be tilted slightly forward while sitting and neutral while standing.

With good posture, completely relax and soften your stomach states Werner. Did you notice how much you were holding it in and how much it expanded? If you didn't notice any change, good job—one less thing to fix.

To fully relax the stomach can be very challenging for most people, especially athletes, because we tend to hold in our bellies the most. Werner works with many athletic people, and when he trains them to relax the stomach completely, most of them physically can't, not because the core is so strong but because they've been subconsciously holding it in for so many years that they don't know how to fully relax their core muscles.

You know your stomach is relaxed if it is soft and you can push four fingers into your abs, toward your spine, with relatively little resistance. Your belly should also bounce back to the resting position without delay.

If it doesn't immediately spring back, you are still engaging your core muscles. When you're able to master relaxing your core, you'll be able to breathe more effectively, and you'll also increase your vital capacity.

When you assume good posture and relax your belly, proper, efficient breathing should happen naturally. To put it all together, stand or sit upright so that your spine maintains its natural curvature.

Relax your shoulders and release all muscle engagement of your core, especially the rectus abdominis muscles. Relax your jaw and face. Slowly inhale through your nose. Allow the breath to move down toward your belly and the rib cage to expand outward.

It should feel like your chest has expanded 360 degrees into your back as well. When the rib cage lifts, your shoulders and collarbones should remain in place. The intercostal muscles that elevate the ribs pull upward toward your collarbones but shouldn't lift them.

The exhalation should be totally passive, meaning without effort or muscular engagement, as the diaphragm returns to its neutral position. Pause at the top of the inhalation and at the bottom of the exhalation.

A great way to slow your breathing is to practice lengthening these pauses. Also, a slower inhalation brings in more nitric oxide. The exhalation should be slightly longer than the inhalation. Count your respiration cycle and aim to slow it to ten to twelve breaths per minute.

If breathing that slowly feels natural, then work on slowing it down even more. If twelve breaths per minute is a struggle to maintain, breathe slightly slower than what feels comfortable.

Consciously breathe like this for fifteen to thirty minutes a day or whenever you think about it, until you have created a new habit of breathing properly. Breathing is life; if we want to be healthy, we need to learn how to breathe well.

> "Each time you breathe out, breathe out all the things in you that keep you from knowing your true self; breathe out all the separateness, all the feelings of unworthiness, all the self pity, all the attachment to your pain. Breathe out anger and doubt and freed and lust and confusion" – Ram Dass

THE AUTONOMIC NERVOUS SYSTEM AND THE POLYVAGAL THEORY

The human nervous system consists of two main parts: The central nervous system includes the brain and spinal cord. The peripheral nervous system comprises the nerves that leave or return to the brain or spinal cord.

The central nervous system is responsible for analyzing all incoming information and stimulation from the body. After deciphering those messages, it sends a response along the peripheral nervous system to the appropriate area in the body.

Most of the information we take in goes directly to the brain for decoding via afferent (incoming) sensory neurons. Then the brain sends out an action signal via the efferent (outgoing) motor neurons.

If the stimulus requires an immediate response, like stepping on a nail or touching a hot pan, the response is dealt with at the spinal cord, and the signal never reaches the brain.

The spinal cord senses information like "hot" or "sharp" and sends a message via the motor neurons, creating an instant reflex loop that tells the appropriate body part to move.

This reaction is known as the reflex arc. The peripheral nervous system branches again into the somatic nervous system and the autonomic nervous system.

The somatic nervous system has two main functions. The first is sensory. It communicates along the afferent pathways, bringing information back to the central nervous system from our sense organs using various types of sensory receptors.

Mechanoreceptors detect changes in pressure, thermoreceptors gauge changes in temperature, and nociceptors sense pain. The somatic nervous system also brings information from our senses of sight, taste, smell, hearing, and equilibrium and then sends the brain a message that paints a picture of our outer and inner worlds.

The second function is to carry signals from the central nervous system along efferent neural pathways to our skeletal muscles for controlled movement.

The autonomic nervous system communicates with our organs and glands. It is responsible for regulating all involuntary and unconscious functions of the body, like digestion, maintaining blood pressure, regulating heart rate, and incognizant breathing.

An easy way to think of it is, the somatic nervous system relays all thinking actions, whereas the autonomic nervous system is for non-thinking functions. The autonomic nervous system divides again into the sympathetic and parasympathetic pathways.

Although these two pathways are mostly antagonistic, they are meant to function concertedly to maintain the regularity of involuntary functions. Changes in our physical, mental, or emotional condition dictate which pathway is dominant.

The sympathetic nervous system is known as the fight-or-flight response, meaning it is more active in response to stressful situations.

The parasympathetic nervous system, also known as "rest and digest," is more engaged when we are in relaxed states such as sleeping and eating. It is also vital for sexual organ function.

With terms like "fight or flight" and "rest and digest," it's easy to think that these two pathways oppose each other, as though one is always fighting for dominance. But in reality, they mostly work with each other in contrast to maintain homeostasis throughout our bodily functions.

What Werner means by working "in contrast" is that the difference between the two helps bring out the aspects of the opposing pathway —like adding black to a painting brings out the brightness of white and the vibrancy of colors.

The autonomic nervous system, through contrasting stimulation or regression of the sympathetic or parasympathetic nervous system, helps increase the opposing effects to maintain homeostasis.

The acute sympathetic response is there for times of extreme danger, but most of the time, we are neither fighting nor running for our lives. Neither are we sleeping or digesting.

We are most often somewhere between these two states. Werner stated that he heard and read many explanations that the two systems function like a switch: when one is on, the other is off.

When we are in a highly stressed state, this might be true, but the body is much more intelligent and complicated than "one is on, and the other is off." In activities such as sexual arousal and ejaculation, the sympathetic, parasympathetic, and somatic nervous systems are all active.

If the primary function of these two systems is to regulate the balance of life-providing functions like pumping blood, controlling blood pressure, regulating hormone secretion, and digesting food, then the on/off analogy doesn't make sense.

A better way of understanding the cooperative roles between the sympathetic and parasympathetic nervous systems is to think of them as hot and cold faucets. When both systems are functioning correctly and one isn't overstimulated, the water is nice and warm.

This balance of the two functioning systems is called autonomic tone. As the situation dictates, more hot or cold water can be added, and when needed, the water can be all hot or all cold.

In reality, though, there is no switch or faucet. Both systems are functioning, releasing hormones and neurotransmitters, titrated as needed throughout the body to handle whatever situation we are experiencing dynamically.

Because so many people deal with chronic stress and, therefore, are in chronic sympathetic activation, the sympathetic nervous system is discussed in a negative way, and probably for good reason. Most people need to learn how to decrease chronic stress and increase parasympathetic tone to bring balance.

But there is another way to look at the sympathetic nervous system, and that is activation and mobilization. When we wake from sleep, sympathetic tone increases. The shift in tone is minor, but we need this activation to get going.

Often we try to aid it by drinking coffee because we are not getting enough rest to restore our baseline. The more activity we do, the more the sympathetic nervous system works to give us the energy we need.

When we start to slow down, the parasympathetic nervous system slowly applies the brakes, and this harmonious relationship continues to support our lifestyle and needs. The sympathetic nervous system originates in the thoracic and lumbar regions of the spine.

Preganglionic nerves exit the spine and connect to the sympathetic chain of ganglion, which are located near the spine. From here, postganglionic nerve fibers travel to organs, blood vessels, and glands.

The postganglionic fibers are myelinated, which enables them to send the signal much faster than unmyelinated preganglionic fibers; this allows the signal to travel to the organs much quicker than it does in the parasympathetic nervous system, where the unmyelinated preganglionic nerves are much longer because the parasympathetic ganglia are located near or within the target organs.

This myelination allows for a quicker sympathetic response. The sympathetic nervous system functions primarily to react quickly to perceived danger or potential threats—i.e., fight or flight. So the bodily response is to mobilize immediately.

The pupils dilate so we can see more, the heart beats faster, and the blood vessels constrict to increase muscle perfusion. The bronchi in the lungs open up so we can breathe better, the adrenal glands release adrenaline, giving us a rush of energy, and urinary and digestive functions are inhibited.

The parasympathetic nervous system (para meaning "around") originates above and below the sympathetic nervous system, in the skull and sacrum. From the brain stem, cranial nerves III, VII, and IX travel to the eyes, face, and mouth, controlling constriction of the pupils, salivation, and lacrimation (the flow of tears).

Cranial nerve X, known as the vagus nerve, travels to the majority of the abdominal organs and viscera. The vagus nerve is the most significant component of the sympathetic nervous system.

It's responsible for slowing the heart rate and contractility, tightening the airways in the lungs, moving food down the digestive tract, limiting inflammation, and helping the immune system.

From the sacrum, parasympathetic fibers connect to the kidneys, bladder, and sexual organs. The parasympathetic nervous system physically functions to aid in rest and recovery, digestion and excretion, and reproduction. The autonomic nervous system's function and influence are significant when it comes to social engagement, mood, and outlook on life.

Stephen Porges developed the polyvagal theory based on the two branches of the vagus nerve that control most of the parasympathetic nervous system: the ventral vagal complex and the dorsal vagal complex.

His approach divides the autonomic nervous system into a three-part system consisting of the ventral vagal complex, sympathetic nervous system, and dorsal vagal complex.

Although the ventral vagal and dorsal vagal complexes both stem from the vagus nerve, they function and respond very differently.

The dorsal vagal complex is responsible for most digestive functions and regulates the organs below the diaphragm. It is the older primal evolutionary branch and is responsible for our earliest stress response, also known as the "freeze" response.

In situations involving a high degree of fear, overstimulation of the dorsal vagal complex can lock us up, rendering us unable to move or act, as we see in many reptiles and some mammals reacting to extreme danger.

When the dorsal vagal complex is in dysfunction, we become withdrawn and antisocial. Increasing the dorsal vagal complex tone calmly and peacefully—i.e., not under danger or stress—brings us into a state of deep relaxation, as we experience in meditation.

The ventral vagal complex regulates the functions of the heart and the respiratory system. It is associated with social engagement and is most dominant when we are healthy and happy.

The polyvagal theory expresses the reactive relationship of the autonomic nervous system in a hierarchical order of safety or danger. The ventral vagal complex, at the top of the system, is related to how we conduct ourselves in a positive manner around others; interact with our friends, family, and strangers; and present ourselves in social situations.

If we sense danger or a threat, then the sympathetic nervous system reacts with the fight-or-flight response. If the situation is perceived as life-threatening, then the dorsal vagal complex reacts with immobilization, dissociation, and shock.

If we are in a place where we feel safe, then stimulation of the sympathetic nervous system moves us toward a healthy state of mobilization where we can work, dance, play, do sports, and physically interact.

The dorsal vagal complex adds balance by bringing us into a state of rest, rejuvenation, and deep relaxation.

In this model, we see the mutable interactions of the autonomic nervous system and the importance of each part's function concerning a healthy and safe state versus reacting to a threat or danger.

The polyvagal theory maps out the response of the ANS when stimulated while feeling safe or feeling stress or danger. In a healthy state of balance, we are primarily stimulating the VVC.

When we experience changes from external or internal stimuli, we can quickly shift from safe to unsafe or vice versa and switch branches of the ANS. We can also get "stuck" in the SNS or DVC if we remain in a chronic state of stress.

HEART RATE VARIABILITY

So how do you know that your nervous system is balanced and regulated? Probably the best way is just to observe yourself:

Do you usually feel stressed or overwhelmed?

How many hours do you sleep each night?

How would you rate the quality of your sleep?

Do you get sick easily or often?

When you are sick, how long does it typically take you to recover?

Do you exercise regularly?

It's easy to know that your nervous system is out of balance if your answers to these questions are not what you'd like them to be. But you can have a low-stress life, sleep well, and rarely get sick and still not have a healthy regulation of your nervous system.

One of the tools used to understand the health of the nervous system is heart rate variability, or HRV. Heart rate variability is a measurement of the distance between heartbeats in milliseconds.

If your heart beats sixty times per minute, it isn't necessarily beating once every second; it is beating an average of once per second. As we breathe in and out, the duration of each heartbeat changes.

This fluctuation exists because inhalations stimulate our sympathetic nervous system; in turn, the sympathetic nervous system speeds up our heart and makes it beat at a more regular and consistent tempo.

However, our exhalations stimulate the parasympathetic nervous system, which causes our heart rate to slow down and our heart rhythm to become more irregular, as though to "breathe" with our respirations, which again is a positive sign of a healthy autonomic nervous system and increased parasympathetic tone.

HRV is a marker of the health of the autonomic nervous system, revealing the relationship between the sympathetic and parasympathetic nervous systems. The lower the HRV number (the more regular and consistent the heartbeat), the more dominant the sympathetic tone is.

The higher the HRV number, the less sympathetic tone. Essentially, our heart breathes along with our breath, which directly affects the nervous system. The higher the variability, the healthier the state of your nervous system.

Because we can make our autonomic nervous system respond by speeding up, slowing down, or changing the depth of our inhales and exhales, our HRV score is only a reliable measurement of the health of our nervous system when it's taken while we're asleep.

However, it is good to monitor how our breath practices are increasing our HRV in real time. Doing breath practices that increase HRV has long-lasting effects, and, in addition to good sleep and low stress, breathing is one of the best ways to regulate nervous system function.

High HRV shows more than just the balance of the autonomic nervous system. It's also an excellent indication of cardiovascular health, the ability to handle stress and exercise, and a high fitness level.

People with high HRV also generally have strong willpower, a calm demeanor, good social engagement, and self-control. Low HRV is related to chronic stress, pain, inflammation, depression, and increased risk of cardiovascular disease, cancer, and death.

THE POLYVAGAL THEORY AND THE IMPORTANCE OF FEELING SAFE

The autonomic nervous system reacts directly to emotion, stress, and how we are breathing. When our perception of our environment switches from feeling safe to feeling scared or anxious, the stress response generates changes in our breathing pattern.

If we reverse the reaction by changing our breathing patterns, we can also change the response of our autonomic nervous system, our associated emotions, and possibly our perception of the environment.

Hopefully, we are not living in a continuous state of stress and fear and do not find ourselves often needing to use the breath to bring us back to a relaxed state.

The polyvagal theory emphasizes the importance of how the autonomic nervous system is stimulated. It makes a clear distinction between how the nervous system reacts if we are feeling safe and how it reacts if we are feeling afraid or threatened.

Feeling unsafe stimulates the sympathetic nervous system and triggers the fight-or-flight response. If the fear is overly intense or the situation seems life-threatening, then the freeze response that is associated with the dorsal vagal complex of the parasympathetic nervous system is triggered.

In contrast, when we feel safe in our environment and activate the sympathetic nervous system, we move toward a mobilization response, where energy to be active, work, play, and socialize is increased.

Even though it is still the sympathetic nervous system being activated, its effect on our emotions and physiology is very different. The same is true when we feel safe in a relaxed state and move into the dorsal vagal complex: we enter into a state where we can rest, repair, digest, meditate, and sleep, as discussed earlier.

The third part of the autonomic nervous system and the other branch of the vagus nerve that is a part of the parasympathetic nervous system is the ventral vagal complex.

Each component of the breath has a direct physiological effect on the autonomic nervous system. The inhalation activates the sympathetic nervous system, which manifests as an increased heart rate. Making the breath quicker and deeper also stimulates a more sympathetic tone.

In turn, exhaling stimulates the parasympathetic nervous system, as evidenced by a decreased heart rate. Slowing the breath down, especially on the exhale, stimulates an even more parasympathetic tone.

"When a practitioner through yogic practices merges the inspired and expired breaths (Prana and Apana Vayus respectively), which are usually out of balance, they neutralize each other. When both airs are neutralized, a single air known as Samana emerges in the abdominal region around the navel area. This energy/air is imperative for awakening and rising the Kundalini. – Santata Gamana

BREATH EXERCISES FOR STIMULATING THE AUTONOMIC NERVOUS SYSTEM

These next six breathing exercises explore how changing the breath, either by speeding it up, slowing it down, or breathing deeper or shallower, has an immediate effect on our nervous system and, in turn, our energy levels and emotional state.

Each component of the breath is linked to our nervous system; therefore, we can stimulate or balance the autonomic nervous system as we see from the direct influence on our heart rate variability.

These exercises can be used to quickly change our mood and energy levels as needed. Each breathing technique is simple and can be done at any time, anywhere.

EXERCISE 1: INCREASING SYMPATHETIC TONE

Take a few moments to breathe naturally and notice your energy level. When you feel ready, inhale fully and quickly through your nose for three to four seconds. After you fill your lungs, open your mouth and sigh to release the breath.

Make sure the exhalation is quicker than the inhalation. Continue for thirty seconds to a minute. Afterward, let your breath return to normal and take a few moments to notice if your energy levels have changed. You should feel a little more energized.

If you practice this breath longer, you'll feel a more significant response.

EXERCISE 2: INCREASING PARASYMPATHETIC TONE

Take a few moments to breathe naturally and notice your energy level; it's okay if you are still feeling energized from the first exercise. Take a slow, moderate inhale through your nose for five to seven seconds.

Slowly exhale through your nose for ten to fourteen seconds. Continue for thirty seconds to a minute. Take a few moments to notice any differences. You should feel more relaxed.

Doubling the length of the exhalation and slowing the breath stimulates a more parasympathetic tone, which slows the heart rate and lowers blood pressure.

EXERCISE 3: BALANCING THE AUTONOMIC NERVOUS SYSTEM

Take a few moments to breathe naturally and notice your energy level. If you are feeling low on energy, do exercise 1 until you start to feel your energy levels rise. If you feel very energetic or anxious, do exercise 2 until you begin to feel your nervous energy diminish.

Once you approach your baseline, inhale through your nose for eight to ten seconds, take a comfortable pause at the top of the inhalation, and then exhale through your nose for eight to ten seconds.

Repeat for one to two minutes to feel the desired effect. Matching the in-breath and the out-breath while also slowing the breath helps regulate the autonomic nervous system and bring us into a more balanced state, stimulating the ventral vagal complex.

Breath retention stimulates the autonomic nervous system in different ways depending on the intensity of the breath-hold, our level of training, and how comfortable we feel while holding our breath.

Adding breath retention after an inhalation or exhalation increases carbon dioxide levels, which stimulates the parasympathetic nervous system. Increasing carbon dioxide levels also facilitates increased oxygen delivery to the cells, and improved cellular respiration increases energy levels.

Breath retention after an inhalation brings us into the ventral vagal complex, leaving us feeling more balanced, and, if paired with breathing that focuses on inhalations, results in more balanced energy.

Holding our breath after an exhalation brings us into the dorsal vagal tone, and we generally feel much more relaxed in ways akin to rest-and-digest.

Breath retention with empty lungs is much more challenging because we have only 1,000 to 1,200 mL of residual air in our lungs for gas exchange, making the need to breathe feel much more urgent.

This urgency can quickly evoke panic and activate the sympathetic nervous system, stimulating the fight-or-flight response, which is never the response we want when doing any type of breathing exercise.

EXERCISE 4: INCREASING BALANCED SYMPATHETIC TONE WITH BREATH RETENTION

Take a moment to establish your baseline. Take a full, deep breath through your nose over three to four seconds. Hold your breath at the top of the inhalation for fifteen seconds.

Open your mouth and exhale quickly with a sigh. Repeat for one to two minutes. Pause for a moment to feel the effects of the practice. This exercise should leave you feeling more balanced and energized with less of an anxious sensation than you might have experienced in exercise 1.

This is because both the sympathetic nervous system and the ventral vagal complex are being stimulated. Try doing exercise 1 and exercise 4 back-to-back to see how the two slightly different practices affect you.

EXERCISE 5: INCREASING PARASYMPATHETIC TONE WITH BREATH RETENTION

Breathe calmly for a few moments. Inhale slowly for five to seven seconds. Exhale for ten to fourteen seconds, and then hold your breath after the exhalation for another ten to fourteen seconds.

Repeat for thirty seconds to a minute. Allow your breath to return to normal and notice the effects of the practice. You may have had two very different responses.

If the breath retention was easy for you, the effect might be a deep sense of calm; if it was challenging, it might result in anxiety or agitation.

With practice, you can maintain a relaxed state and parasympathetic tone, even adding breath retention after the exhalation where you feel extremely challenged.

EXERCISE 6: BOX BREATHING

This exercise focuses on creating equal lengths through all four parts of the breath. Inhale for a count of five. Hold your breath after the inhalation for a count of five. Exhale for a count of five.

Hold your breath after the exhalation for a count of five. Repeat for five to ten rounds. This exercise is great for balancing the autonomic nervous system and stimulating ventral vagal tone, resulting in a balanced, equanimous state.

> *"When the breath is unsteady, all is unsteady; when the breath is still; all is still. Control the breath carefully. Inhalation gives strength and a controlled body; retention gives steadiness of mind and longevity; exhalation purifies body and spirit" – Goraksasatakam*

ASTHMA AND TOXIC ALLERGY TRIGGERS.

Those with Asthma (or anyone else thinking they are heathy) should be wise and cautious of the triggers that cause attacks. Some triggers are food additives, aspirin (Tylenol, Advil etc.) MSG and sulfites. In your home mold grows on shower curtains, bathtubs, tiles etc. Dust mites favorite areas are blankets, pillows, carpets, stuffed toys etc.

Asthma can be triggered by smoke from the burning end of the cigarette or second-hand smoke. Do not smoke at home and do not allow others to smoke in your home.

Cockroach body parts and droppings may trigger asthma attacks. Cats and dogs dander are triggers. Nitrogen Dioxide gas can irritate eyes, nose, throat and may cause shortness of breath. This gas comes from appliances that burn gas, wood and kerosene, such as BBQ's, fireplaces and car exhausts.

Chemical irritants and fragrances (buy only odor-free) can also be triggers! These are found in soaps, detergents, fabric softeners, cleaners, perfumes, aftershaves, colognes, deodorants, hairsprays, mothballs, candles, air fresheners etc. The lung's enemy is found in most people's homes.

Go to the gym all you want, eat salads every day all you want, your overall health will still not be optimal if you are breathing daily the dangerous substances that are found in your home, which are deemed normal in our modern-day society. Blood is the river of life, if you keep breathing toxic and dangerous substances your blood will be polluted which means every part of your body will be polluted.

THE CORRECT WAY OF BREATHING

This is one of the many breathing methods, we cover various breathing exercises in our blog articles. Put one hand on your belly and the other on your chest. The diaphragm is located between the chest and the abdomen. If you want to know exactly where it is located, put one hand in front of your mouth, a few cm/inches away from it. While the other hand is placed on your belly.

Now, pretend that the hand that is in front of your mouth is a candle and try to push the breath out as if you were trying to blow out a candle. When you do that, you will feel a contraction in above your belly, and it's where the diaphragm is. Okay, since now you know the exact location of the diaphragm, keep the hand where you felt the diaphragm and the other on your chest.

First inhale deep with your belly/diaphragm until your belly swells/becomes bigger where you cannot put any more oxygen in your diaphragm. But don't exhale yet. Continue breathing with your chest until you cannot breathe anymore and then exhale slowly until your lungs empty completely. So, by performing a full inhale and exhale you are performing a full breathing (and exhaling) cycle.

Filling up both the diaphragm and chest with oxygen is the correct full breathing technique that you should perform constantly. At first you might forget to do this on a regular basis, so to remind yourself write a few little notes and stick them on your fridge, room door, car's dashboard, on your phone etc.

Be in the moment, and to achieve that, you should practice DEEP CONSCIOUS BREATHING as explained previously. It is not difficult at all to perform it as you were born with that basic ability, you just forgot it in the early years of your life.

"Anything you think that is away from the moment, it will turn you into a prisoner of memories (past) and imagination (future)."

We could live hundreds of years if we breathe properly, eat properly (fasting is a must), think properly, behave, and feel properly. Every single breath not taken correctly damages you. The damage is accumulative.

Breathing is automatic, and most people take it for granted. You brush your teeth, you walk, you run, you drive a car, or you create art (the process of it, not the actual creativity that requires thinking) or many other things you do in your life. When you learn something of doing it without thinking about it, that is an automatic habit.

The way you breathe, controls your life, your look, your energy, your emotions and your resistance to diseases. It controls your very life span.

Bibliography and references

The Illuminated Breath by Dylan Werner

Super Power Breathing by Paul C. Bragg and Patricia Bragg

Body Mind Soul – As You Believe So Shall It Be by Saimir Kercanaj

The Tao Of Health, Sex and Longevity by Daniel Reid

TAKE CARE OF YOUR
M I N D

*"The mind is everything,
what you think, you become"*

USE IT OR LOSE IT

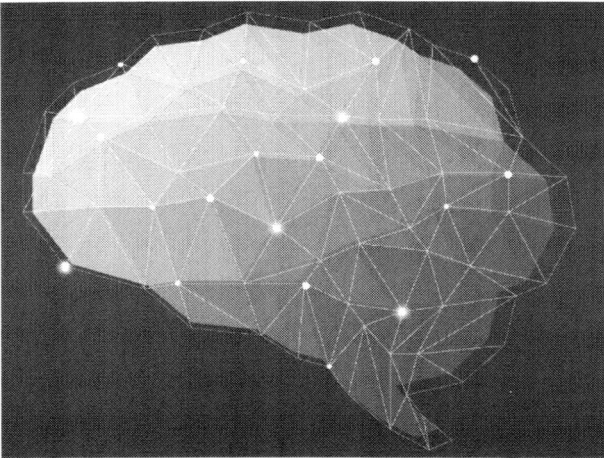

6

ARE YOU A STUDENT OR A TEACHER?

"The student and the teacher are mirrors of each other. They cannot progress without one another. The student helps the teacher progress as a student. The teacher helps the student to become a better teacher." - Rimias K. Neo

WHEN THE STUDENT SEEKS the path leading to higher knowledge, he should not omit to fortify himself; throughout his work, with one ever present thought. He must never cease repeating to himself that he may have made considerable progress after a certain interval of time, though it may not be apparent to him in the way he perhaps expected. Otherwise, he can easily lose heart and abandon all attempts after a short time.

The powers and faculties to be developed are of a most subtle kind, and differ entirely in their nature from the conception previously formed by the student. He had been accustomed to occupying himself exclusively with the physical worlds. The physical world is but a fraction of the true reality, and yet even the true reality may be an illusion. Regardless of the illusion, if you think something is real, then it is real to you on a micro level. As long as the student knows that the physical body is one side of the coin (the other side being the spiritual self) the student will definitely be on the right path to enlightenment. Enlightenment happens daily anyway, incrementally but when you are self aware in everything you say or do, then enlightenment gains momentum.

"Education is not preparation for life; education is life itself." - John Dewey

The world of spirit and soul had been concealed from his (*men/ women - hijacked/corrupted humanity*) vision and concepts. It is therefore not surprising if he does not immediately notice the powers of soul and spirit now developing in him. In this respect there is a possibility of discouragement for those setting out on the path to higher knowledge, if they ignore the experience gathered by responsible investigators. The teacher is aware of the progress made by his pupil long before the latter is conscious of it. He knows how the delicate spiritual eyes begin to form themselves long before the pupil is aware of this, and a great part of what he has to say is couched in such terms as to prevent the pupil from losing patience and perseverance before he can gain knowledge of his own progress. The student often doesn't know that he is a teacher.

We all are both teacher and student at the same time. We often doubt ourselves because we compare with others. Comparing with others is fine for the purpose of being inspired to improve our daily lives but it is not good when we become envious. We are each other; would you be envious of yourself? Then you shouldn't be envious of anyone else either.

The teacher as we know, can confer upon the pupil no powers which are not already latent within him, and his sole function is to assist in the awakening of slumbering faculties. But what he imparts out of his own experience is a pillar of strength for the one wishing to penetrate through darkness to light. Many abandon the path to higher knowledge soon after having set foot upon it, because their progress is not immediately apparent to them.

"When you try to do one step forward to attain knowledge about the hidden truths, then do the same time three steps forward to perfect your character." - Rudolf Steiner

And even when the first experiences begin to dawn upon the pupil, he is apt to regard them as illusions, because he had formed quite different conceptions of what he was going to experience. He loses courage, either because he regards these first experiences as being of no value, or because they appear to him to be so insignificant that he cannot believe they will lead him to any appreciable results within a measurable time. Courage and self-confidence are two beacons which must never be extinguished on the path to higher knowledge. No one will ever travel far enough who cannot bring himself to repeat, over and over again, an exercise which has failed, apparently, for a countless number of times.

Long before any distinct perception of progress, there rises in the student, from the hidden depths of the soul, a feeling that he is on the right path. When you get distracted here and there, you end up going nowhere. You will still go there, but first you will be humbled by the "NOWHERE." In darkness you will learn how to see. In darkness you will nurture your third eye, in darkness you will see the LIGHT.

"When the student is ready the teacher appears. When the student is truly ready the teacher Disappears." - Lao Tzu

INTERNAL AND EXTERNAL TEACHERS

You cannot become a painter if you refuse to handle a paint-brush. Likewise, you cannot receive esoteric training if you are unwilling to meet the demands considered necessary by the teacher. There are two teachers, internal and external ones. Lessons in life come from within but also from others, from real teachers but also from regular people you meet daily. Any experience is your teacher. You are the alchemist; you decide what you do with the ingredients (advice). You have free will and you and only you must exercise it. Never let anyone decide on your behalf. If that happens then it would mean that you gave away your gift/power (free will).

Your body/mind/spirit is the most precious gift you were ever given. It is a pity for yourself to go wasted. The gift was not given to you just so you can do what you want without regarding the rest of the world. Through the actions you take with your body and your mind you either inspire yourself and the world or you destroy yourself and the world. There are consequences for abusing or neglecting the gift/ magic. Be an example that inspires those around you to be on the righteous path. Do that and you will be rewarded. The rewards I'm talking about are beyond material riches. They are eternal rewards that are priceless such as an open mind, an open heart, being in the moment, appreciating all life forms and much more. Be willing to constantly learn from others, no matter how unintelligent others may seem to you, rest assured that everyone has something to teach you, whether they are intelligent or ignorant.

7

THE ALLEGORY OF THE CAVE

THIS MUCH-DISCUSSED (and much-misunderstood) story is a key part of Plato's *Republic*, a work which has the claim to be the first ever literary utopia.In *The Republic*, Plato and a number of other philosophers discuss the ideal society, focusing on education, political leadership, and the role and responsibility of the individual within society.

The Allegory of the Cave represents a number of the core ideas of Plato's thinking in one short, accessible parable. But what is the meaning of this allegory? Before we offer an analysis of Plato's idea, here's a summary of what he says about it in *The Republic*. One of the key ideas on Plato's *Republic* is his theory of forms, where 'forms' means much the same as 'ideas'. And the Allegory of the Cave represents Plato's approach to ideas. We are invited to imagine a group of people sitting in an underground cave, facing the walls. They are chained up and they cannot move their heads. Behind them, a fire is forever burning, and its flames cast shadows onto the cave walls.

Between the fire and the cave walls, there is a road, and people walk along this road, carrying various objects: models of animals made of stone and wood, human statuettes, and other things. The people who walk along the road, and the objects they carry, cast shadows on the cave walls. The people who are chained in the cave and facing the wall can only see the shadows of the people (and the objects they carry): never the actual people and objects walking past behind them.

To the people chained up in the cave, these shadows appear to be reality, because they don't know any better. Reality, to these people chained in the cave, is only ever a copy of a copy: the shadows of the original forms which themselves remain beyond our view. But someone comes and unchains the people in the cave. Now they're free. Let's say that one of them is set free and encouraged to look towards the fire behind him and his fellow cave-dwellers. He can now see that the things he took for reality until now were merely shadows on the wall. But this knowledge isn't, at first, a good thing. The revelation is almost overwhelming.

The light of the fire hurts his eyes, and when he is dragged up the slope that leads out of the cave, and he sees the sun outside, and is overwhelmed by its light. In time, however, he comes to accept that the sun is the true source of light in the world, the cause of the seasons and the annual cycle of things. And he would come to feel sorry for those who remain behind in the cave and are content to believe that the shadows on the cave wall are reality. Indeed, the people who remain behind in the cave believe he wasted his time in going outside and simply ruined his eyes for nothing.

But the man who has been outside knows there is no going back to his old beliefs: his perception of the world has changed forever. He cannot rejoin those prisoners who sit and watch the shadows on the wall. They, for their part, would resist his attempts to free them, and would sooner killer him than be led out of the cave, as he was. And so, if the man who has seen the sun returns to the cave, his eyes will take time to adjust back to the darkness of the cave and to the shadows on the wall. He will now be at a *disadvantage* to his fellow cave-dwellers, who have never left the cave and seen the light.

Analyzing "The Allegory of The Cave

An allegory is a story that has a double meaning: as THE PENGUIN DICTIONARY OF LITERARY TERMS AND LITERARY THEORY puts it, an allegory has a primary or surface meaning, but it also has a secondary or under-the-surface meaning. This is certainly true of Plato's Allegory of the Cave. But what is its secondary meaning?

Although THE REPUBLIC is classified as a work of philosophy, it is structured more like a dialogue or even a play (though not a dramatic one), in that it takes the form of a conversation between several philosophers: Socrates, Glaucon, Plato himself, and a number of other figures are all 'characters' in the REPUBLIC. The Allegory of the Cave, as Plato's comments indicate, is about the philosopher seeing beyond the material world and into the 'intelligible' one. The symbolism of the cave being UNDERGROUND is significant, for the philosopher's journey is upwards towards higher things, including the sun: a symbol for the divine, but also for truth (those two things are often conflated in religions: Jesus, for example, referred to himself as 'the way, the truth, and the life' in John 14:6).

Plato insists, however, that the philosopher has a duty to RETURN to the material world, to the world of the cave and its inhabitants (or PRISONERS), and to try to open their eyes to the truth. It is no good leaving the cave behind. The philosopher must return down into the cave and face ridicule or even persecution for what he has to say: he has to be prepared for the unpleasant fact that most people, contented with their mental 'chains' and their limited view of the world, will actively TURN on anyone who challenges their beliefs, no matter how wrong those beliefs are. People come to love their chains, and being shown that everything you've believed is a lie will prove too much (as Plato acknowledges) for many people, and even, initially, for the philosopher. (It is curious how prophetic Plato was: his teacher and friend Socrates would indeed be ridiculed by

Aristophanes in his play "The Clouds" and later he would be put on trial, and sentenced to death, for his teachings).

In other words, those people who have seen the ideal world, have a responsibility to educate those in the material world rather than keep their knowledge to themselves. So, we can see how Plato's Allegory of the Cave relates not only to the core ideas of THE REPUBLIC, but also to Plato's philosophy more broadly. There are several further details to note about the symbolism present in the allegory. One detail which is often overlooked, but which is important to note, is the significance of those objects which the people on the road are carrying: they are, Plato tells us, human statuettes or animal models carved from wood or stone.

Why is this significant? These objects cast their shadows on the walls of the cave, and the people chained in the cave mistake the shadows for the real objects, because they don't know anything different. But the objects THEMSELVES are copies of things rather than the original things themselves: statues OF humans rather than real humans, and models OF animals rather than the real thing. So, as Robin Waterfield notes in his excellent notes to his translation of Plato's REPUBLIC, the objects are 'effigies' of real things, or reflections of TYPES. This means that the shadows on the wall are reflections of reflections of types, therefore.

So (as Waterfield puts it) the shadows on the wall might represent, say, a kind of moral action, while the objects/statues/effigies themselves are a person's thoughts on morality. When these thoughts are observed in the material world (i.e., on the cave wall), we are observing a moral action somebody has taken, which reflects some moral code or belief. Without a moral compass we are doomed to death, literal and metaphorical. In today's society people can travel (by car, airplane, train) to long distances. On the surface seems like freedom.

To a certain extent it is. Most of these people travel not for pure joy but for some kind of trophy as in going to weddings, parties, vacations to get away from the prison they have created where they live. But when they get back from those long trips, they get back to the same prison for them to complain again that life is so unfair. No such a thing as unfair, you must work toward your own liberation. If you get dirty, you will not clean yourself up unless you look at yourself. Other people have their own dirt to clean up, some may tell you that you are dirty, but nobody will tell you *"Here, you are dirty, I'm going to clean you up"*. Nobody can save/liberate you. You have to save yourself and you can only do that after you realize that you are inside the prison of your own thoughts.

Bibliography

The Republic Of Plato by Allan Bloom and Adam Kirsch

https://interestingliterature.com/

8

ATTENTION AND SELF-OBSERVATION

"If one wants to get rid of this or that undesirable psychological element, first of all, one has to learn to observe with the purpose of obtaining a change; because, certainly, if one does not learn to self-observe, any possibility of change becomes impossible" - Samael Aun Weor

OBSERVATION: DIRECTED ATTENTION

IN HIS BOOK *KUNDALINI: THE SACRED FIRE OF ALL RELIGIONS*, Samael Aun Weor stated that first of all, we must begin by comprehending the need to know how to observe. We are, for example, sitting here, all of us, in these chairs; we know that we are sitting, but we have not observed these chairs.

In the first case, we have the knowledge that we are sitting on them, but observing them is already something else. In the first case, there is one, let's say..., there is knowledge, but not observation. Observation requires a special concentration: Observe what they are made of, and then go into meditation, discover their atoms, their molecules... This already requires, let's say, directed attention...

Knowing that one is sitting in a chair is undirected attention, passive attention; but looking at the chair would already be directed attention.

Likewise, we can think a lot about ourselves, but this does not mean that we are observing our thoughts; observing is different, it is different...

We live in a world of inferior emotions. Anything produces inferior emotions in us, and we know that we have them; but it is one thing to know that one is in a negative mood, and another thing to observe the negative mood one is in, which is something completely different...

Let's see, for example, on a certain occasion, a gentleman told a psychologist, he said, "Well, I feel antipathy for a certain person, and he quoted his name and surnames.

The psychologist replied, "Observe that person."

The interrogator answered again, he said, "But how am I going to observe that person, when I know that person?"

The psychologist concluded that he did not want to observe, that he knew, but did not observe; knowing is one thing and observing is quite another thing: one can know that one has a negative thought, but that does not mean that one is observing it; one knows that one is in a negative mood, but one has not observed that negative mood...

In practical life, we see that within us there are many things that should cause us shame: ridiculous comedies, inner questions, protests, morbid thoughts, etc.; but knowing that you have them is not having observed them.

Someone can say: "yes, right now I have a morbid thought"; but it is one thing to know that you have it and another thing is to observe it, which is totally different.

So, if one wants to get rid of this or that undesirable psychological element, first of all, one has to learn to observe with the purpose of obtaining a change; because, certainly, if one does not learn to self-observe, any possibility of change becomes impossible...

When one learns to self-observe, the sense of self-observation develops in oneself. Normally this sense is atrophied in the human race, it is degenerated, but as we use it, it unfolds and develops.

As a first point of view, we come to evidence through self-observation that even the most insignificant thoughts, or the most ridiculous comedies that happen internally and that are never externalized, do not belong to our essence, they are created by others: by our "I's."

What is grave is to identify oneself with those comedies, with those ridiculous things, with those protests, with those angers, etc., etc. If one identifies with any inferior extreme of these, the "I" that produces them becomes stronger, and thus, any possibility of elimination becomes more and more difficult. So, observation is vital when it comes to bringing about a radical change in ourselves...

The different "I's" that live inside our psyche are very cunning, very sagacious; many times, they appeal to the "roll" of memories that we carry in the intellectual center...

Let us suppose that in the past one was fornicating with any other person of the opposite sex, and that one is insisting, or not, in eliminating lust; then the ego of lust will appeal, it will seize the center of memories of the intellectual center; that "I" will grab there, let's say, the "roll" of memories, of scenes of lubricity and he will pass them off as the person's fantasy, and he will become more invigorated, he will become stronger and stronger.

Because of all these things, you must see the need for self-observation. Therefore, a radical and truly definitive change would not be possible if we did not learn to observe ourselves...

Knowing is not observing; thinking is not observing either. Many believe that thinking of oneself is observing but it is not. One can be thinking of oneself, and yet one is not observing oneself; Thinking of oneself is as different from observing as thirst is from water, or as water from thirst!

THE OBSERVER AND THE OBSERVED

Weor stated obviously, one must not identify with any of the "I's." To observe oneself, one has to divide oneself into two, in two, in two halves: a part that observes and another part that is observed.

When the observing part sees the ridiculousness and nonsense of the observed part, there is possibility of a change...of discovering (suppose the "I" of anger)...that this "I" is not us , that he is he; we could exclaim: "that "I" has anger; I have no anger, but that "I" has it! Therefore it must die, I am going to work on it to disintegrate it"...

But if you identify with anger and say, "I am angry, I am furious!" Anger becomes stronger, more and more vigorous, and then how are you going to dissolve anger, in what way? You couldn't, right?

So, you shouldn't identify with that anger, or with his tantrum, or with his tragedy, because if one becomes identify with his creation, well, one ends up living in that creation as well; and that is absurd.

As one works on oneself, one goes deeper and deeper into the issues of self-observation, one goes deeper and deeper; In this, even the most insignificant thought must be observed; any desire, however temporary at it might be, any reaction, must be a reason for observation, because any desire, any reaction, any negative thought, comes from this or that I.

And if we want to create light, liberate the soul, are we going to allow those "I's" to continue to exist? That would be absurd!

But, if what we want is light, if we are truly in love with light, we have to disintegrate the "I's", there is no other choice but to turn them into dust. And we could not turn to dust what we have not observed; then we need to know how to observe.

INTERNAL CHATTER VS SILENCE OF THE MIND

In any case Weor stated, we also have to take care of internal chatter, because there are many negative, absurd inner dialogues; inner conversations that never are exteriorized; and naturally, we need to correct that inner chatter, to learn to keep silent: "to know how to speak when one should speak; and to know how to keep silent when one should keep silent." This is the law, not only for the physical world or the exterior world, but also for the interior world.

These negative inner chats, later, come to externalize physically; That is why it is so important to eliminate inner negative chat, because it harms (you have to learn how to keep inner silence)...

Normally it is understood by "mental silence", when one empties the mind of all kinds of thoughts, when one achieves stillness and silence of the mind through meditation, etc.

But there is another kind of silence: let us suppose that a case of critical judgment is presented before us, in relation to a fellow man, and nevertheless, mentally we remain silent, we do not judge, we do not condemn; we shut up both externally and internally; in this case, then, there is inner silence.

The facts of practical life, after all, must be kept in close correspondence with a perfect inner conduct. When the facts of practical life agree with a perfect inner conduct, it is a sign that we are already creating, in ourselves, the famous mental body.

If we put the different parts of a radio of those of a tape recorder, for example, on a table, but we don't know anything about electronics, then we won't be able to capture the different "soundless" vibrations that swarm in the cosmos either; but if by comprehension we put the different parts together, we will have the radio, we will have the device that can pick up sounds that we would not otherwise pick up.

Likewise, the different parts of these studies, of this work, complement each other, to come to form a wonderful body, the famous body of the mind. This body will allow us to better capture everything that exists within ourselves and will develop in us (more), the sense of intimate self-observation; and that is quite important.

Thus, the object of observation is to make a change within ourselves, to promote a true, effective change.

THE STEPS TO ELIMINATE DEFECTS

Once we have become, shall we say, skillful in self-observation states Weor, then the process of elimination becomes possible. So, there are, properly speaking, three steps in this matter:

First - *observation*
Second - *critical judgment*
Third, *which is properly the elimination of this or that psychological "I".*

When observing an "I", we must see how it behaves in the intellectual center, in what way, and know all its "games" with the mind; second, in what way is it expressed through feeling, in the heart; and the third, to discover his mode of action in the lower centers (motor, instinctive and sexual).

Obviously, in the sexual center, an "I" has one form of expression, in the heart it has another form, in the brain another. In the brain, an "I" manifests itself through the intellectual matters, namely, reasons, justifications, evasions, loopholes, etc., in the heart as a suffering, as affection, as a love apparently many times (when it is a question of lust), etc., etc.; and in the motor-instinctual-sexual centers, it has another form of expression (as action, as instinct, as lascivious impulse, etc., etc.).

For example, let's cite a specific case: lust. An "I" of lust, before a person of the opposite sex, in the mind may manifest itself with constant thoughts; It could manifest itself in the heart as an affection, as an apparently pure love, clean of all stains, to such an extent that one could perfectly justify oneself and say: "but well, I do not feel lust for this person, what I am feeling is love".

But if one is observant, if one is very careful with one's own machine and observes the sexual center, one comes to discover that in the sexual center there is a certain activity before that person; then one comes to evidence that there is no such affection, or love, let's say, there is no such love for that person, but lust is what there is. Behold how fine the crime is: lust can perfectly disguise itself, in the heart, with love, compose verses, etc., but it is disguised lust...

If one is careful and observes those three centers of the human machine, one can see that it is an "I"; and already discovering that it is an "I", having known its "behavior" in the three centers (that is, in the intellectual, in the heart and sex), then one proceeds to the third phase.

What is the third phase? It is the execution! It is the final phase of the work: execution! Then one has to appeal to prayer at work. What is meant by "prayer at work"? Prayer at work must be done on the basis of intimate self-remembering.

> *"You must comprehend the process of lust, which is the worst enemy of the elimination, the worst enemy of the dissolution of your ego"* - Samael Aun Weor

Bibliography

Kundalini: The Sacred Fire Of All Religions by Samael Aun Weor

9

THE FULL AWAKENING IS THE END OF THE PREVIOUS IGNORANCE

WHAT DOES THE TITLE OF THIS CHAPTER MEAN? Think of it this way, when you were in the first grade at school, you were learning things until the time for the exam. After you graduated, you thought you accomplished something big, not knowing that you had so much more to learn. Or when you were a baby in the womb, you had to grow for nine month (technically, 40 weeks equals 10 months, based on *13 months/28 days each month* in one year calendar) and then when you were born it seemed like you were liberated from a prison not knowing that while in your physical body you had so much more to learn such as: talk, walk, think, love, work etc., for you to find out that you got out of one prison and entered another. Feel free to replace the word 'prison' with school. After you live a physical life for decades, you pass away (change form energetically) and as a spirit you think finally you are free and fully awakened since you escaped the physical dense 3D world/life. For you to find out that school was never finished, there are more grades or trials for you to go through. Never lie to yourself by thinking that you are fully awakened. If you were fully awakened, then you would have no drive/will of doing anything, you would have no reason to live. The fact that we are striving to learn more about ourselves and creation as a whole means that we are on the right track.

A cat would not bother with a dead or an almost dead mouse or a chipmunk. A cat is excited to chase something that the cat wants to work for and not something that is ready without having to put any effort. The same applies to us, at least to those that are putting effort in becoming better versions of themselves (you are one of them), we want to earn something, we do not want it handled to us. Another example if you are a male is, men want to work toward conquering women, we don't want them to be easy. Men like to chase and not be chased. Again, I'm speaking of men that know themselves, men that honor their masculinity. Otherwise, the balance between the sexes would be weak as we see it in our society where many get together for convenience, some for money/materialism and some for pleasure. But that's another subject for another time.

Anytime you think you are intelligent, you are taking one step backward because thinking like that, puts you in a comfortable state of mind. When the mind is comfortable, you become lazy. When you are lazy you have no drive to exercise, to research and act on things that matter the most in our lives which are mastering ourselves, connecting with our higher selves, connecting with nature, help one another etc. Unite for a better present and future as opposed to gossip, backstab, lie, cheat, worry, fear, kill/hurt, deceive etc.

THIRTEEN – From the book GAIN WISDOM THROUGH PRACTICED KNOWLEDGE by Rimias K. Neo

The 13th missing (actually the 11th one as per the right order) month "Undecimber" may seem foreign to you but anything that you are comfortable with up to this point in life, it was foreign to you at one point in the past. By now you know that this system that we are in is messed up, it is obvious that it is. Consider different information that contradicts this sick, and corrupt system that people have been suffering under. Based on the 13-zodiac calendar, if you were born between November 22-December 21 you are Ophiuchus. To play it safe, practice the long fast (3.5days), no sex/lust etc., every time there is a full moon (13 times a year), regardless of which zodiac sign the Moon is at, whether your date of birth falls on one sign based on the 12-month calendar or if it falls under a different sign based on the 13-month calendar. Especially for women that they won't have to go through the monthly menstrual period if the body/mind readjusts to a 13-month calendar cycle. Since everything begins and ends in the mind, your body/emotions will never be healthy and balanced if your mind is chaotic internally. You have a conscious and subconscious mind. You may think that you are happy (whatever this word may mean to you), but your subconscious has a different story to tell. The subconscious never lies. It will tell what you feed it. You may look at yourself in the mirror and think "That's me". That is not who you are. Who you are cannot be seen with your physical eyes.

In a chapter about consuming meat, I wrote that many people who consume animal meat will keep consuming and thinking they are consuming healthy food because they will compare it with the 3D lab printed meat. The same logic may apply here, by comparing these 13-zodiac dates with the fake ones you may think that these make sense. These dates could still be wrong, even though a year has to have 13 months/13 zodiacs. I am saying this so that you do not blindly believe anyone (including me). I have done my research; you should do your own research. There is no doubt that the 12-month calendar/zodiac dates that we were used to all life, are fabricated/lies.

No matter how true something is, it is still a lie if you do not realize it to be the truth. Realization is not something that comes from the rational mind but from within, from your heart, from your cells/DNA and from the depth of the pit of unlimited cosmic knowledge. Regardless of the dates, you can awaken and raise your kundalini either way, but in those specific days, combining it with the Moon's entrance in your Sun/Zodiac sign, the potency of it is much higher. When you become a decent practitioner in fasting, then you can begin fasting, no sex (no orgasm/no ejaculation for men), no alcohol etc. every times there is a full moon regardless of your zodiac/Sun sign. Women's only equivalent to losing their life force like men's ejaculation is 'menstruation'.

Orgasming is fine (only if it is a result of tantric sex) for women, women too excrete secretions, the secretions stay inside the body, healing them. Only men lose when they ejaculate. Different people are at different stages of purification/cleansing. Not everyone is capable of fasting right away for 3-4 days at a time, let alone repeating this 13 times a year. The cleaner you are, the lighter your body will be which means you will receive more light in you, in every cell, therefore you can last longer without food, sex etc. First begin to fast for 3,5-4 days when the Moon enters your zodiac sign (12-month calendar dates), then try the same on the 13-month calendar dates. For the dates for each zodiac sign (for each month of the year) when you have to practice the super conscious awakening and for more elaboration on the importance of practicing the kundalini awakening check these books:

Gain Wisdom Through Practiced Knowledge by Rimias K. Neo

2024 *Regeneration Calendar* by Kelly Marie-Kerr

You Are The One by Pine G. Land

DO NOT HAVE ANY SURGERY WHEN THE MOON IS IN YOUR ZODIAC SIGN.

Astrology is very important in human biology. You must have heard about the Hippocrates Oath which all physicians must take so they can uphold specific ethical standards. In his original Oath, Hippocrates said that "if a medic is not an astrologer", he is not worthy to be called a medic". These last words of him from the whole original Oath have been conveniently taken out/erased by the medical mafia. To be an astrologer/medical practitioner is important because the Moon affects the internal organs, depending on which zodiac sign/constellation the Moon is at. When the Moon is in a zodiacal sign/constellation, it stimulates the blood. For example:

When the Moon is in Libra, it influences the kidneys, urinary bladder, veins and the skin. When the Moon is in Aries, it influences the head, teeth, arteries and the tongue. When the Moon is in Cancer, it influences the stomach, breasts, womb and the ovaries. If you had surgery when the Moon is in your zodiac/Sun sign for example when the Moon is in Cancer, there will be complications if you have a surgery in your stomach, the womb, or the ovaries.

If you are Aries and you have a surgery on the head, or teeth you could bleed to death, especially if you had a head surgery. The third cause of worldwide deaths is because of the mainstream so-called medical system. A lot of complications and deaths in the medical field happen because of this one single important thing that they don't practice which is "ASTROLOGY". The mainstream doctors are not taught astrology. If they were taught astrology, then the medical mafia (big pHARMa) would not exist. They profit from people being sick and slowly dying. So, if you have to have any surgery, arm yourself with knowledge. Go to the website *www.mooncalendar.astro-seek.com* and check which organs are influenced by the Moon, based on each zodiac sign or check Tamo's book TO BE REBORN, which has this information plus both the tropical and sidereal dates for 2025; the dates when one should practice the Sacred Secretion or the Kundalini awakening.

Even if you don't have to have surgery, by knowing which organs are influenced by the Moon, you'll know when to take care of your body, in case any of your organs are giving you trouble. For example, if you have discomfort in your stomach, you would fast if the Moon was in your Sun sign, instead of having a big meal and drinking. As a rule of thumb, fast anyway, whenever the Moon is in your zodiac sign. That is what I do. If you have to have surgery and the doctors (legal murderers) book your surgery on the days when the Moon is in your zodiac sign, you can refuse it and rebook it for when the Moon is on a different zodiac sign. Do not feel obligated. You are responsible for your health. They only need money. You are just a product to them and not a sentient being. The best medicine exist already within yourself.

COLLATERAL TEACHING

Ever heard of "collateral damage?" We will talk about the opposite of this. This is about helping as opposed to damaging someone. An example of how to teach someone without even talking to them is to do things in their presence. If you have a child that needs to lose weight, then you walk every day in the house, run, go up and down the stairs. If you do this many days, a seed will be planted in his mind.

Depending on how strong they are, they may water the seed while they are with you, or at a later time. Just try to remember how many things you do or don't do because of repetitions from your parents that you had to go through when you were a child or as a young adult. Governments or corporations are not your friend, we are just digital numbers in their eyes, you are something to be used and disposed of.

The government is also a corporation, so is the Name and the LAST NAME on your legal documents. The legal documents have expiry date. Do you expire? No, you don't. The documents do, but you are not the legal documents. You are a living breathing sentient being. The sooner we honor our divinity, the sooner we will leave ignorance behind us.

Bibliography
Limitless Potential by Saimir Kercanaj
Gain Wisdom Through Practiced Knowledge by Rimias K. Neo
You Are The One by Pine G. Land

10

LIFE IS PHILOSOPHY

WE CAN COMPLAIN ALL WE WANT, but every moment of our lives we have the possibility and potential to love, care and help one another. All it takes is to analyze ourselves and we can then see that life is not as difficult as we make it out to be. Life is "philosophy". We are drown in a world full of lies and deceit but underneath it all lies the Great Truth, that truth is – *"Thinking for ourselves and loving one another."*

> **"If lies didn't exist, then there would be nothing to philosophize about. Everything is philosophy. Duality breeds philosophy, it breeds critical thinking if one develops self-awareness or defeat, passiveness and obedience if one wants to just exist rather than live their life to their full potential."** from the book *Limitless Potential: Journey To Self-Realization* by Saimir Kercanaj

Do fish philosophize why they don't have limbs or why they have to swim? Of course not, fish or animals operate by instinct, they don't have a rational mind like humans. Having a rational mind is both a blessing and a curse for many. When you understand life, life is a comedy to you, meaning that you laugh at the intricacy and at the same time simplicity of life. You laugh because you know that all this convolution is simple and yet people become miserable when they don't think for themselves which in this case life becomes a tragedy. The worst tragedy is when we lie to ourselves. We constantly find excuses as to why we struggle, we would blame anything and anyone but ourselves. The longer we lie to ourselves, the steeper the path becomes. When the path becomes steeper we must put more effort than before, otherwise we would take one step forward and two steps back. No matter how much knowledge you gain, it will still contribute to your struggling if you let your heart to continue being on vacation. Your heart and your mind must work coherently, in tandem. They are best friends. Did you know that your heart has neurons just like your brain? You heart doesn't exist just to pump blood. Life has about 40 thousands neurons. The heart never lies, the mind does.

Whether you are a man or a woman, your life is a philosophy, a successful or a failed one depending on the perception of the world or yourself that you have. Although the world is in direct proportion of who you are individually, but also collectively all of us are responsible for what happens in the world. Some of us are directly affecting the outcome of humanity's life and some affect it indirectly for example the habits that we have. Many women support mega corporations in being consumerists of branded materialistic clothes, gadgets etc (even though this applies to both genders), many men watch porn or are distracted with other meaningless self-destructive habits such as drugs, alcohol, sports etc.

In the book *YOU ARE THE ONE* by Pine G. Land she states:

"As a man you must build every day, you must create every day, you must be your natural authentic self. If you don't, you will succumb to instant gratification in the form of meaningless sex & masturbation, liquor, fantasy screen time (videogames, TV shows, movies etc), and many others foolish activities that will rob the soul out of you. Build a hobby. Build a career, only if it has to do with helping freeing humanity, otherwise any other career offered by the mainstream establishment is only to divide and conquer us. Build your body and your mind. Not many men build their knowledge, even fewer build a passion. Many men go weeks, months and years without building anything because they are defeated mentally/ emotionally/spiritually. They waste their life away. Don't be that man, be better. Do better. Unleash/honor your masculinity so that women feel safe and protected where children and any generation after will have a bright future."

The above talks about men because the chapter was about men, but it applies to both genders.

Usually, men live in the head. That's' how men are wired, at least that's how they operate since chaos took over. Women are the caregivers, the nurturers. Women are the amazing Goddesses that lead men into their hearts. Without women, men would only live in their head (without men, women have no protection). When you live in your head, meaning when you over analyze everything, when your mind is in chaos, you are easily taken advantage of, you can easily be controlled by the small group of beings that control this realm behind the curtains. And no, that is not the government. The government is simply the supervisor, not even the manager.

Regardless who controls what, you have the power to be in charge of your life. Governments will exist for as long as world's population remains ignorant of their own powers. Life is simple when you take a step back and see the bigger picture. When you live in the chaos of the mind, you cannot see far away, you can only see the wall that you create with your assumptions, obedience and refusal to work on your powers/talents and abilities.

Bibliography

You Are The One by Pine G. Land

Body Mind Soul – As You Believe So Shall It Be by Saimir Kercanaj

WARRIOR'S MEDITATION

"Silence is the warrior's art – and meditation is his sword. With it, you'll cut through your illusions. But understand this: the sword's usefulness depends upon the swordsman" – *Dan Millman*

11

WHY MEDITATE?

MEDITATION IS AN ESSENTIAL PREREQUISITE for attaining kundalini, chakra, and higher conscious activation. Delving into the profound essence of one's being necessitates the practice of meditative stillness. By cultivating a tranquil state of mind and emotions, one can cultivate a profound sense of peace and harmony.

For men who choose to retain their semen, directing their focus towards meditating on the movement of their sexual energy through the meridian channels, chakras, and up the spine becomes paramount. Remember, energy follows the path of attention.

Meditation helps to dispel lustful thoughts and desires that may arise after a few weeks of retention. While everything discussed on this blog [*www.theserpentsway.com*] is crucial for awakening the sacred serpent, we emphasize that sexual energy retention and transmutation form the foundation, with meditation following closely in importance.

The genuine importance of meditation is found in the inner evolution that occurs by cultivating the mind. Hence, the purpose of any meditation approach is to revolutionize the mind.

It is common for our minds to be burdened with troubles. We often find ourselves preoccupied with distressing thoughts, overwhelmed by anxiety or anger, and affected by the hurtful actions of others.

During these challenging moments, we yearn for the ability to control our emotions and gain mastery over our minds, ultimately freeing ourselves from the grip of these tormenting feelings.

Through meditation, we can cultivate and enhance positive human qualities just like we do in other forms of training in arts and skills. It involves developing a clear perspective and bringing out the good qualities that lie dormant within us.

In Meditation, the mind takes center stage. At present, it is in a state of simultaneous confusion, agitation, rebellion, and influenced by numerous conditioned and automatic patterns.

The objective of meditation is not to silence or numb the mind, but rather to set it free, bring clarity, and establish equilibrium. According to Buddhism, the mind is not a distinct entity, but rather an ever-changing stream of experiences, a continuous flow of conscious moments.

Although these experiences can be accompanied by confusion and suffering, we also have the capacity to embrace them with a state of clarity and inner freedom. Our current suffering stems from mental confusion, which hinders our ability to think clearly and make sound decisions.

The solution lies in developing an accurate understanding of reality and transforming our mindset. Our ability to eradicate the main sources of suffering hinges on our understanding and resolution of the mental poisons: ignorance, aggression, greed, pride, and jealousy.

These poisons are a direct result of our self-centered and delusional attachment to the ego. By breaking free from this attachment, we can pave the path towards a life devoid of suffering. Buddhism identifies multiple categories of suffering.

While visible suffering is observable, hidden suffering is connected to impermanence and change, occasionally masking itself as pleasure. A more profound and less conspicuous suffering originates from our fundamental ignorance, enduring as long as we are trapped in delusion and selfishness.

The ultimate aim of meditation is to attain the skill to free all individuals from suffering and enhance their overall well-being. Throughout our extensive journey on 'The Way', we have explored numerous forms of meditation.

These include both guided and unguided practices. For those new to meditation, I highly recommend starting with guided meditation, as it was instrumental in my own meditation journey. Fortunately, there are countless guided meditation resources available on YouTube.

When it comes to meditation, there are different approaches to achieve calmness and gain insight. Techniques such as focused attention, body scan, and energy meditation are commonly used. Personally, I prefer to start my meditation sessions with a five-to-ten-minute warm-up using focused meditation.

During this warm-up, I find a quiet, dark room and focus my attention on a candle. This practice not only helps me prepare mentally, but it also has a powerful effect on stimulating the third eye. Other types of meditation include visualization, resting awareness, reflection, Zen, mantra, transcendental, and kundalini meditation.

A vital component of any spiritual path towards higher consciousness is shadow work. This practice involves delving into the depths of our unconscious to uncover the aspects of ourselves that we are currently unaware of.

It encompasses all the suppressed attributes, attitudes, impulses, and qualities that do not align with our self-identity, and brings them to the forefront. By engaging in shadow work, we can bring disowned material to light and learn to accept our traits, impulses, and attributes.

As meditation plays a crucial role in both kundalini awakening and self-mastery, we will extensively explore a wide range of meditation techniques, including shadow work, in our blog.

This is because we believe that meditation is an essential aspect of personal growth and spiritual development. Expect a wealth of information on different meditation techniques. Now, let's transition to a highly impactful technique that I discovered a couple of years back known as the Warrior's Meditation.

> *"Meditation is not a way of making your mind quiet. It's a way of entering into the quiet that's already there – buried under the 50,000 thoughts the average person thinks every day" – Deepak Chopra*

Meditation and Concentration

The Warrior's Meditation, a hidden gem in the realms of self-improvement, cognitive enhancement, and stress relief, is passed down by a Master of Four Samurai Arts. Richard L. Haight is an expert instructor in martial arts, meditation, and healing arts.

He started his martial arts training at the young age of 12 and later traveled to Japan at 24 to further his skills with renowned masters in various disciplines. Over his 15 years in Japan, Richard earned master's licenses in four samurai arts and a traditional healing practice known as Sotai-ho.

To paraphrase Haight, nearly all forms of meditation adhere to a specific and rigid structure that defines their essence. However, solely relying on form-based definitions of meditation can lead us to prioritize the rituals and conventions, thereby overshadowing the original intention of meditation, which is to cultivate a heightened state of mindfulness and self-discovery.

To evade the limitations imposed by form and tradition, Haight redefined meditation as not merely a form, but rather as a state characterized by a vibrant clarity that emerges from a deep integration of being fully aware in the present moment. The means by which we arrive at this state of vibrant present awareness is of secondary importance when compared to the direct experience of this vivid clarity.

In order to go beyond form and tradition, one must begin by identifying the fundamental principles of consciousness. Understanding the brain's activity during meditation, in contrast to its activity at rest, can provide valuable insights into isolating these principles. These distinctions manifest in observable brainwave patterns.

The brain exhibits beta waves when it is attentive and immersed in mental tasks. For instance, a regular conversation would induce the standard beta wave activity in most people. Conversely, disagreements, public speaking, and debates would induce an elevated beta wave activity.

In general, most people have their brains constantly producing measurable beta waves unless they are at rest. When in a state of rest, the brain usually emits slower and higher amplitude alpha waves. Alpha waves signify a non aroused state, hence a simple calming meditation would align with alpha.

Once we have isolated, experienced, and comprehended the variances between beta wave and alpha wave, and their significance in meditation, and have also grasped the fundamental principles of meditation, we will start our investigation into the basic Total Embodiment Methodology practice, known as the Warrior's Meditation.

Buddhists believe that all meditation practices stem from either Vipassana "insight" meditation or Samatha "purification" meditation. While meditation predates Buddhism, the core principles of Vipassana and Samatha can be found in both ancient and contemporary meditation techniques.

In English, Vipassana is typically translated as insight, while Samatha is translated as purification. The core concept of Vipassana can be best described as awareness, while for Samatha, concentration is a suitable term.

In the Buddhist sutras, it is mentioned that the Buddha taught Vipassana and Samatha together, highlighting them as attributes rather than separate meditation methods, crucial for attaining liberation.

Regrettably, despite the assertions made by various Buddhist schools about teaching the authentic meditation of Buddha, the original technique remains unknown due to the absence of any original writings.

Nevertheless, contemporary manifestations of Buddhism have distinctively categorized Vipassana and Samatha, formulating specific meditation practices. The majority of schools predominantly engage in concentration-based meditations, specifically Samatha, which seamlessly align with religious customs.

These practices often revolve around a sutra, prayer, religious image, or name, serving as the focal point. When it comes to meditation, Vipassana is generally seen as a less rigid practice than Samatha.

In Samatha, the focus is on complete concentration on a single point, whereas Vipassana offers a more adaptable approach. For instance, concentration techniques may involve focusing on a specific object or repeating a mantra, while mindfulness meditation encourages observing the breath and thoughts without getting caught up in them.

Apart from Buddhism, we discover that most meditations practiced globally belong to the concentration category, differing mainly in their focal point, tradition, and cultural background.

Mindfulness meditation, a secular form of Buddhist practices, exemplifies the principle of Vipassana/awareness. By directing attention to the natural rhythm of the breath, our awareness expands beyond what it would be with mantra meditation.

From the Total Embodiment Methodology viewpoint, the fundamental Samatha/concentration and Vipassana/awareness meditations are quite similar, as both emphasize exclusive attention. Samatha schools recommend complete focus, while Vipassana schools are slightly less strict in their approach.

These schools are exclusive in their meditative focus because when you fully concentrate on one thing for an extended period, your mind will eventually calm down, leading to a profound shift into a deeper state of awareness.

Traditional meditations like Samatha or Vipassana are distinct in their focus compared to the Total Embodiment Methodology approach, as they are centered on concentration.

By experiencing concentration firsthand, you will grasp the key distinction between the TEM method and other meditation techniques. To provide you with this essential experience, Haight crafted a concentration-focused meditation for you to try out immediately, drawing from traditional practices.

When examining various types of meditation practices from around the world, a common thread emerges: the emphasis on concentrating on a specific focal point while excluding all distractions.

For instance, Zazen in Zen Buddhism emphasizes maintaining proper physical posture, while mindfulness meditation centers on following the natural flow of the breath. Mantra-based meditations like Transcendental Meditation and Christian meditation involve repeating a spiritual word either aloud or silently. Despite differences in origin, religion, or technique, all meditative practices share this common focus.

Let's now gain some practice in concentration meditation. You have the freedom to choose any focal point that suits you. It could be your body, your breath, the third eye situated slightly above your eyebrows in the center of your forehead.

For our practice, we will adhere to the commonly recommended principles followed by the majority of meditation traditions.

Time
Set a timer for 15 minutes to ensure a peaceful meditation experience free from time constraints.

Place

Pick a warm, serene, and cozy place where you can concentrate without any disruptions. I always choose to meditate in total darkness. I also like to burn incense during my meditation sessions, although it is not mandatory.

Positioning

Find a comfortable position to practice in, ensuring your spine is gently upright without being too rigid. I have always chosen to sit in a comfortable chair during my meditation practices instead of assuming the traditional cross-legged posture, due to my involvement in weight-lifting and extreme biking riding.

Eyes

Keep your eyes shut or slightly open, but if they're open, refrain from focusing on any specific object in front of you.

Practice

The main objective of your meditation practice is to sustain your awareness on the chosen focal point, while striving for utmost relaxation. Whenever you observe your mind wandering, which is bound to happen occasionally, effortlessly redirect your attention back to the focal point without any worry.

Don't let yourself be excessively preoccupied with getting it right or wrong, as this worry will hinder your ability to fully relax and achieve a meditative state.

"Every time you create a gap in the stream of mind, the light of your consciousness grows stronger. One day you may catch yourself smiling at the voice in your head. This means that you no longer take the content of your mind all that seriously, as your sense of self does not depend on it" – Eckhart Tolle

Biblioghraphy:

The Warrior's Meditation by Richard L. Haight

12

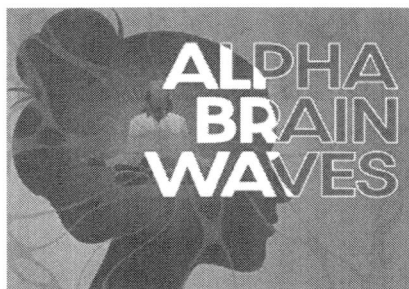

SHIFTING TO ALPHA

WHEN WE BEGIN our meditation practice, the very first change that occurs can be observed in our brainwaves. Initially, our brainwaves are in a beta state, associated with an active and focused mindset.

However, as we enter into a meditative state, these brainwaves shift to alpha waves, indicating a state of relaxation and calmness. Surprisingly, this transition from beta to alpha waves typically happens within a minute of starting our meditation session.

The alpha wave intensifies as we spend more time practicing engaged meditation, eventually progressing into theta, delta, and potentially even gamma waves. These waves indicate deeper levels of awareness and can bring about numerous health advantages.

It has come to light that any form of meditation can bring about a shift in brainwave patterns, specifically to the alpha state. Remarkably, by dedicating just one minute to sitting and attentively observing your breath, you are likely to enter the alpha wave.

Similarly, engaging in a minute of prayer or chanting can yield the same outcome. With the awareness that any meditation practice can lead us to the alpha state, we can harness this knowledge to develop a straightforward technique for efficiently shifting our brains to the alpha wave, even while engaged in our daily activities.

Utilizing vagal breathing can easily transition most individuals into alpha wave with just a few breaths. To accommodate varying levels of anxiety and stress, it is advisable to practice a minimum of six vagal breaths to ensure everyone successfully makes the shift to alpha.

Once we become acquainted with the Warrior's Meditation, we won't depend on breath techniques anymore. Nevertheless, vagal breathing will provide you with a glimpse of how effortlessly you can transition from beta wave to alpha. Once you can identify this transition, we can explore more applicable approaches that seamlessly fit into your daily life.

Before delving into vagal breathing, it is essential to grasp the concept of the vagus nerve: the vagus nerve's name is derived from the term vagabond, which translates to "wanderer," due to its role as the longest cranial nerve with sensory fibers connecting the brainstem to visceral organs.

This nerve governs the parasympathetic nervous system, mitigating the impact of an overactive sympathetic nervous system, which includes symptoms like stress, anxiety, and fight-flight-freeze responses, along with specific forms of depression.

The vagus nerve controls numerous essential functions by transmitting sensory and motor signals to the organs. Traditionally, the medical field did not recognize any link between the immune system and the nervous system due to the different nature of immune and nerve cells.

This led to the belief that the nervous system had no impact on immune responses through vagus nerve stimulation. However, ongoing research by Kevin Tracey is suggesting that stimulating the vagus nerve could be an effective treatment for chronic inflammation and diseases considered incurable.

Tracey utilized electricity to activate the vagus nerve, however, we can achieve the same effect by harnessing the power of our breath. Wim Hof's groundbreaking research has demonstrated that individuals who practice his unique breathing technique possess an extraordinary immunity against harmful toxins introduced into their bloodstream.

Initial research conducted at the Radboud University Medical Center in the Netherlands suggests that Hof's method may have the ability to temporarily inhibit an inappropriate immune response. Similar results have also been observed with other breathing techniques.

In order to assess Hof's innate immune system response, Pikkers and Kox employed a different experiment. This immune system is designed to differentiate between the body's own cells and foreign invaders, effectively eliminating the intruders.

To stimulate an immune response, they administered an endotoxin. Following exposure to the injected toxin, the majority of subjects experienced symptoms like fever, headaches, and shivering, as well as increased cytokine levels.

Unlike the control subjects, Hof did not suffer from any negative symptoms and had lower cytokine levels. His students displayed a response similar to Hof's in subsequent tests.

The connection to the vagus nerve is likely the key factor, as it is being influenced by specific breathing patterns. While additional research is essential to uncover the reasons behind the immune-enhancing effects of these breathing techniques, the research on the vagus nerve and its impact on overall health is continuously expanding.

The research by Kevin Tracey revealed that the vagus nerve, which is connected to every organ in the body except the adrenal glands, plays a crucial role in preventing inflammation.

When the vagus nerve detects an inflammatory signal, it communicates with the brain, leading to the production of anti-inflammatory neurotransmitters that help regulate the immune response. Practices such as vagal breathing can support the immune system in mounting a suitable defense against pathogens.

By transmitting electrical signals, the vagus nerve facilitates communication between your gut and brain, allowing for the interpretation of your "gut feeling" or intuition. When the communication is optimal, our gut feeling is more reliable, whereas an over-reactive or under-reactive nervous system can lead to inaccuracies.

The vagus nerve plays a crucial role in connecting with and regulating the function of all organs, including the heart. By sending electrical impulses to the muscle tissue in the right atrium, it effectively controls the heart rate.

This process leads to the release of acetylcholine, which in turn slows down the pulse. Tibetan monks have demonstrated this ability through their breathing techniques, and you can also achieve the same effect.

The vagus nerve triggers the body's relaxation response. Many individuals experience an overactive sympathetic nervous system, leading to continuous secretion of stress hormones like cortisol and adrenaline.

By practicing proper breathing techniques, you can activate the vagus nerve to promote relaxation by releasing acetylcholine, prolactin, vasopressin, and oxytocin. Regularly stimulating the vagus nerve has been found to greatly diminish or even stop symptoms of rheumatoid arthritis, hemorrhagic shock, and other serious inflammatory illnesses that were previously thought to be untreatable.

Here's how to perform vagal breathing:

Aim

The purpose of this exercise is twofold: to transition from beta wave to alpha wave and to be aware of the exact moment when this transition takes place.

Preliminaries

Prior to starting the vagal breathing exercise, observe the current state of your mind and the sensations in your body. It is unnecessary to attempt to alter the sensations in your body beforehand, as the main objective of the exercise is to observe any changes that occur during the exercise.

Time

Start your timer for fifteen minutes in order to fully grasp the concept of vagal breathing through experience.

Position

It is important to note that Valsalva maneuvers can result in fainting, which is why it is recommended to sit without using a backrest during this exercise to minimize the risk.

Eyes

Start with your eyes closed to get a feel for the process, then feel free to open them whenever you're ready.

Breathing Method

Inhale deeply and hold your breath, using it to gently expand your lungs and create a pleasant sensation. By adjusting your posture and body alignment, you can manipulate the airflow within your lungs. Experiment with different directions of pressure to discover which one feels most comfortable in the present moment.

If you enjoy stretching in one direction for a few seconds before switching to another, feel free to do so. Remember, the key to a transformative experience lies in embracing the sensations rather than overthinking the process.

The crucial aspect of vagal breathing is not about being overly determined, but rather about being mindful of what brings comfort at every step of the way. By practicing vagal breathing correctly, by focusing on what truly brings pleasure, the brain will transition from beta to alpha waves with the very first breath.

After just fifteen minutes of practice, you will experience a significant release of tension from your body, leaving you with a soothing, serene sensation.

Dealing with Distraction

If you find your mind drifting, which is highly improbable if you are truly savoring the experience, simply redirect your attention to your breath without any worry.

"Inner stillness is the key to outer strength" – Jared Brockk

The Awareness Paradox

Concentration meditations all have the same goal: to concentrate on a single point while blocking out all other distractions. This point of focus can vary, but we will focus on either a candle flame or a fixed point on the wall.

Fixed-Point Focus Experiment

The objective of this experiment is to direct our full attention towards a candle flame, a specific spot on the wall, or a chosen point of interest, for an extended period of time.

To ensure accurate results, we will be conducting our experiment a minimum of two times. When performing the fixed-point focus exercise for the first time, remember to set your timer for a duration of five minutes.

Find a cozy spot to sit, either in front of a wall or at a table with a candle. Pick a specific point on the wall or light the candle a few feet away. Start your timer and concentrate on the candle or the fixed point.

Focus your gaze solely on the fixed point or the flickering candle flame, disregarding everything else around it. Be cautious not to strain your eyes by squinting, as this may hinder your ability to perceive the bigger picture. Take a moment to conduct the experiment before proceeding.

What did you notice?

The majority of individuals, upon being asked this question, often express that they attained a sense of tranquility throughout this experiment. However, it is completely normal if you felt anxious or did not encounter a state of calmness, as that is not the main objective of this experiment.

The exercise clearly shows that you inevitably take in the whole peripheral vision when you are consciously alert and your eyes are open. It's paradoxical because trying to block out sensory awareness actually means you are consciously aware, and a conscious person will always be aware of the complete visual field.

It's likely that during your initial attempt, you were unknowingly observing the entire visual field while attempting to ignore it. If you didn't realize this paradox during the first experiment, there's no need to be concerned. To provide further clarity, we will conduct the same experiment again, this time utilizing a stopwatch instead of a timer.

Commence your stopwatch and initiate a concentrated gaze, and take note of the duration it takes for you to become aware that you cannot disregard the entirety of the visual field.

Chances are, you quickly grasped that you can't avoid seeing the entire visual field. It's like being told not to think of purple monkeys – you'll inevitably think of them, just as you can't help but perceive the whole visual field even when you try not to. While it may seem trivial initially, you'll soon realize it's the secret to transformative, versatile, liberating meditation.

What is the functioning mechanism of the principle?

Ponder over the countless times you've engrossed yourself in a book, oblivious to anything beyond its confines or the particular sentence captivating your focus. Alternatively, if reading isn't your forte, recall the instances when you've watched a movie without registering anything beyond the screen. The fact of the matter is that you did observe, but the memories slip from your grasp.

Let us clarify. Your eyes perceive all the visible light spectrum that enters your field of vision – encompassing the entire movie screen or book, as well as everything beyond their borders that is still within your eyesight. However, you just don't retain the memory of what your eyes have seen.

Confirm our claims by consulting any book. Focus solely on the content within its pages, ignoring everything outside its borders. Avoid the temptation to cheat by bringing the book too close to your face, limiting your peripheral vision. You'll soon realize that you can't help but look beyond the book as you read.

Were you able to comprehend the text you were reading? It might come as a surprise to some that they struggle to understand the text when they are aware of what is happening in the room around them. However, after dedicating enough time to practicing the Warrior's Meditation, you may find that reading while maintaining spatial awareness is not as challenging as it initially seems.

The connection between this experiment and meditation is worth exploring.

The experiment highlights the contrast between our conscious awareness and lack thereof. In a state of conscious awareness, we naturally perceive everything that enters our senses.

However, when we find ourselves in a semi-unconscious, dreamlike state, such as when engrossed in movies, books, or lost in our thoughts about the past or future, we are unable to remember or utilize information that is not directly related to our current focus. Despite our senses receiving this additional information, it remains inaccessible to us.

To delve into the intricacies of perception, we can turn our attention to the two hemispheres of the brain and their distinct roles. In the case of approximately 90% of the population who are right-handed, the left hemisphere functions as a serial processor, while the right hemisphere operates as a parallel processor. However, it's worth noting that there are exceptions to this pattern, such as left-handed individuals, whose hemispheres may exhibit reversed functions.

The majority of the population, around ninety percent, are right-handed individuals. Their sense of self, time, logical thinking, language skills, and access to specific knowledge are mainly situated in the left hemisphere, known as the serial processing brain. On the other hand, their spatial awareness, creativity, bodily awareness, and more are primarily located in the right hemisphere, which is the parallel processing brain.

A major drawback of the serial processor, located in the left hemisphere, is its inability to handle more than one conscious action simultaneously. Nonetheless, it compensates for this limitation by offering a highly detailed perception of the selected object through its exceptional focusing capability. Concentration, a primary talent of the serial processor, is essential for human survival, but it can be physically exhausting and induce stress.

Regrettably, the serial processing hemisphere lacks awareness of the surrounding context beyond its focal point. The Samurai were aware that focus and thinking demand significant energy, leading to slower combat response times.

The Samurai saw thinking as a function of the "mind." By training diligently to enhance their skills, they unlocked the potential of reaching a state of "no mind" that was incredibly effective in warfare. They strived to consciously access "no mind" in order to eventually utilize its strengths unconsciously.

They were actually preparing themselves to strategically tap into the capabilities of parallel processing (right hemisphere), which can handle multiple information simultaneously at faster speeds compared to serial processing, albeit with lower resolution.

The Samurai were able to tap into the parallel processor through meditation, but they probably didn't have knowledge of the specific brain region responsible. However, understanding this detail is not essential to achieve the desired functionality valued by the Samurai.

Some left-handed individuals may feel inclined to believe they utilize the parallel processing hemisphere more than right-handed individuals. However, it is important to note that the hemispheres can interchange functions. Therefore, left-handed people usually engage in serial processing, self-awareness, and rational thinking just like right-handed individuals.

The way our brains are organized ensures that even if we lack training, our daily experiences are primarily influenced by the hemisphere responsible for generating our thoughts and sense of self, regardless of whether we are left-handed or right-handed. This fact is evident as left-handed individuals still possess a sense of self and do not have any advantage in terms of movement or meditation.

Having gained familiarity with the serial processing hemisphere, it is time to delve into the intricacies of the parallel processing hemisphere. As previously mentioned, the parallel processor has the remarkable capability to handle multiple tasks concurrently, albeit at faster speeds and with reduced resolution compared to the serial processor.

Overall, the parallel processor functions as a sensory warning mechanism, persistently overseeing the information received through our senses, even when our conscious perception may not be fully attentive to all of it.

The serial processor and the parallel processor have contrasting ways of perceiving information. While the serial processor follows a linear approach, the parallel processor decodes information at a much faster pace, using abstract methods that hold significant meaning. The perceptions of the parallel processing brain are complex and challenging for the serial processor brain to comprehend.

One of the key functions of the parallel processor is to control our body's awareness and movements. During dream and sleep states, we experience meandering, distorted, and non-linear perceptions, which are characteristic of the hemisphere responsible for parallel processing.

Through conscious awareness training, the elite Samurai uncovered the ability to synchronize with the parallel processor. This enabled them to utilize information at a heightened speed compared to their thinking mind, resulting in enhanced awareness, movement quality, and efficiency.

The elite Samurai were driven by the desire for enhanced battlefield performance. However, their training also facilitated a connection between their conscious and subconscious minds, resulting in heightened awareness, improved martial arts skills, and an overall better quality of life.

This led to the emergence of exceptional Samurai known as "sword saints," who surpassed the abilities of ordinary warriors in ancient Japan. Kamiizumi Ise no Kami, the esteemed founder of Shinkage-ryu, was widely recognized as a sword saint.

The fixed-point focus experiment demonstrates that awareness cannot avoid being aware, as it lacks the ability to filter out information. By focusing our minds and attempting to exclude information, we actually encourage both hemispheres to work together and share information within our perception. The amount of information we can recall is greatly influenced by practice.

This focusing technique poses a major drawback. It becomes clear that the brain fatigues rapidly under such intense focus. For a warrior, preserving energy efficiency is vital, hence in Total Embodiment Method, we adopt an alternative approach.

By exploring the awareness paradox, we discover that concentration can expand our awareness, if we recognize its value. Once we reach this level of awareness, we no longer need to maintain intense focus. Knowing about the paradox liberates us from fixating on specific objects or thoughts.

Merely understanding that we cannot actively exclude sensory data allows us to explore new horizons in our meditation practices, enabling us to utilize our senses as a pathway to inner transformation and improved physical, mental, and emotional vitality.

With an understanding of the awareness paradox, we can delve into the possibilities presented by our senses. Imagine harnessing the senses in a manner that leads to profound meditative clarity. By embarking on a sensory meditation journey, we can break free from the constraints of concentration, stillness, and isolation. Gone would be the days of seeking a perfect environment devoid of interruptions for meditation.

What we've learned is that the secret lies in shifting our approach to utilizing our senses. In the context of Total Embodiment Method, the fundamental principle is to avoid concentrating on one thing and instead embrace a broad awareness that encompasses all directions and all senses.

Surprisingly, expanding all senses without prejudice leads to a profound understanding of both internal and external aspects, fostering a connection to all life. The sense of proprioception, which defines our body's boundaries in space, becomes more fluid rather than rigid.

This openness results in enhanced tranquility and clarity. Broadening awareness of the senses transforms the brain, enhancing perceptual adaptability, deepening insight, and improving overall well-being.

> "Detach yourself from all that makes your mind restless.
> Renounce all that disturbs its peace. If you want peace,
> deserve it. By being a slave to your desires and fears,
> you disturb peace" – Nisargadatta Maharaj

Biblioghraphy:

The Warrior's Meditation by Richard L. Haight

13

CONSCIOUS SIGHT, HEARING, OLFACTION, TASTING AND FEELING

FROM MY OWN PERSONAL EXPERIENCE, I have found that engaging in conscious sight, hearing, olfaction, tasting, and feeling is most enjoyable when done in the comfort of your own backyard or out in nature. Out of these five senses, conscious sight holds a special place in my heart. While conscious hearing is also quite remarkable, it is conscious sight that truly ignites the state of mind that athletes often describe as being in the 'zone'.

Science has yet to reach a consensus on how sight functions, despite our extensive knowledge on the subject. Certain aspects of visual perception continue to baffle researchers.

The enigma of vision lies in the fact that the human eye cannot generate images of high enough quality to enable us to navigate the world solely based on the information it provides. It is widely believed that the brain compensates for this deficiency by supplementing the missing information with relevant memories.

This theory suggests that a significant part of our visual understanding is essentially a biological assumption. If this theory is accurate, it sheds light on the various visual deceptions that we humans tend to fall for. If you're not familiar with visual illusions, do a quick internet search for "Optical Illusion" to understand what I mean.

It is believed that visual perception is the outcome of the eye capturing light from the visible spectrum that bounces off objects. Subsequently, the brain decodes the electrical signals transmitted by the eye to construct the mental images of our surroundings.

Light enters the human eye through the cornea and is then directed by the lens onto the retina, a light-sensitive membrane located at the back of the eye. Within the retina, there are two types of photoreceptive cells: rods, which detect shades, and cones, which detect color.

These cells convert light particles, known as photons, into electrical signals. The optic nerve carries these signals to different areas of the brain, including the central ganglia, visual cortex, and superior colliculus. In these regions, the signals are interpreted and combined with experiential association, specifically memory.

To enhance our meditation practice, it's essential to grasp the concept of vision being divided into two distinct types: foveal vision and peripheral vision. Foveal vision involves the detailed, color-rich perception that is concentrated along the central line of sight. This type of vision is predominantly used by contemporary humans, especially when engaging in tasks such as reading.

Peripheral vision encompasses the visual field outside the direct line of sight. It is characterized by low-definition and color-insensitive vision. Despite these limitations, peripheral vision is highly sensitive to shades and movement, making it a valuable asset for maintaining awareness. Hunter-gatherers heavily rely on their peripheral vision during their daily activities.

Peripheral Viewing Exercise

The awareness paradox teaches us that trying to exclude information from our visual awareness actually prevents us from doing so. It's energy-consuming to focus on excluding information, so it's better to pay attention to the whole visual field. In this chapter, we will meditate by directing our attention to the entire visual field without trying to focus or exclude anything.

Time

Start your timer for 15 minutes. Even though most people's brains switch to alpha after only one minute of peripheral viewing, dedicating 15 minutes to practice will give you a deeper insight into the changes that peripheral viewing brings about within you.

Position

Find a peaceful spot where you can relax undisturbed and get comfortable. This activity can be done effortlessly whether you choose to do it inside or outside but optimal conditions are found outdoors.

Aim

The purpose of this exercise is to utilize our peripheral vision to intentionally connect with the parallel processor through an alpha brain wave. This practice can enhance our awareness, reduce stress, and promote a peaceful state of mind. Before beginning, take note of your emotions. Additionally, observe the moment when you transition to alpha state during the exercise, and reflect on your feelings upon completion.

Eyes

Direct your gaze forward and observe the entirety of your visual field. Most people have a horizontal field of view of almost 200 degrees and a vertical field of view of about 100 degrees, creating a visual field shaped like "binoculars." Keep in mind that the center of the visual field offers the highest visual resolution, with full color and detail. When we concentrate on the center of the visual field, we are utilizing foveal vision.

To optimize our conscious awareness, it is crucial to acknowledge the awareness paradox, which highlights the significance of foveal vision in excluding unnecessary information. However, in order to conserve energy, we need to adopt an alternative approach with our eyes.

The key is to concentrate on the outer edges of our visual field, also known as peripheral vision. Although peripheral vision may lack high resolution and vivid colors, it excels in detecting shades and motion. By giving importance to peripheral vision, we can tap into the parallel processing capabilities of our brain, a technique that the Samurai discovered.

Stargazing exemplifies the power of peripheral vision, showcasing its ability to detect the subtle glimmering of stars in our peripheral vision. Interestingly, when we attempt to concentrate on a faint star, it becomes more challenging to perceive.

Despite our primary focus on central vision, our brain is continuously receiving input from the peripheral field of vision. This selective attention mechanism helps us ignore peripheral visual information that is not relevant to our immediate task, such as when we are immersed in watching a movie at the theater.

Watching a movie can be considered an unconscious activity since we often lose track of our surroundings. Total Embodiment Method focuses on being aware of the present moment and space. While it's okay to get lost in a movie occasionally, it's important not to make foveal vision our default way of seeing things.

Once you become accustomed to perceiving the entire peripheral field of vision, take some time to truly relax and fully appreciate the sensations that arise from this expanded awareness. As you delve deeper into this state, you may start to notice slight changes in the way you perceive colors, time, and space.

In fact, you might even feel a sense of euphoria, as if you were in an altered state of mind. While these experiences may bring pleasure to many, they are not the primary focus of this meditation. The true aim of this practice, as well as any TEM meditation, is to cultivate a heightened sense of contextual awareness in our lives. This enables us to align ourselves more harmoniously with the entirety of reality.

Developing a natural instinct for being aware of our entire visual field is extremely beneficial, as our eyes are constantly in use throughout our active daily lives. This heightened awareness will keep you from constantly feeling out of sync and in a stressed state, allowing you to remain conscious and focused.

With practice, you'll notice a decrease in stress levels and a greater ability to handle uncertainty. The more you practice, the more you'll be uplifted from negative emotions. The significance of conscious visual awareness should never be overlooked.

"Meditation is the dissolution of thoughts in eternal awareness or pure consciousness without objectification. Knowing without thinking; merging finitude in infinity" – Swami Sivananda

Conscious Hearing

By engaging in the peripheral viewing exercise, you have already realized the immense potential of using your entire visual field for meditation. However, it may come as a pleasant surprise to learn that the sense of hearing can also be harnessed in a similar manner.

The way we perceive sound is actually quite different from what we might assume. As sound waves make their way into the outer ear, they pass through the ear canal and cause the eardrum to vibrate. These vibrations then influence three small bones in the middle ear, namely the malleus, incus, and stapes.

Sound vibrations are magnified by the three bones and then sent to the cochlea; a snail-shaped organ filled with fluid in the inner ear. Within the cochlea, the basilar membrane divides it into upper and lower sections, serving as the base for essential hearing structures.

When vibrations inside the cochlea cause the fluid to ripple, a wave travels along the basilar membrane, where sensory hair cells on top of the basilar membrane are moved by the wave. The pitch of the sound is detected according to where the hair cells are on the membrane. The cells in the lower part of the cochlea detect higher-pitched sounds, whereas cells in the upper part of the snail-shaped cochlea detect lower-pitched sounds.

The movement of hair cells caused by the wave results in the interaction between microscopic hair-like projections on their tops and the cochlea's structure. This interaction causes the opening of channels located at the tips of the hair cells. As a result, chemicals rush into these openings, generating electrical signals. These signals are carried to the brain by the auditory nerve. Once the brain receives these electrical signals, it produces sound that we recognize based on our associated memories.

Essentially, what we think of as hearing is actually more like an illusion created by the brain when it is stimulated by electrical signals from the auditory nerve. Think about every movie that you have ever watched. All of the sound effects were probably produced by things other than what you see on the screen.

For example, in old movies, horse footfalls might have been made by clacking together two dried coconut husk halves. Hearing the clacking, your brain just assumes that it is a horse walking on asphalt. Even if you didn't know it was a horse movie and were unable to see any video, just hearing the coconut halves clacking together, your brain would probably conjure the image of a horse to fit the sound.

Our brain plays a crucial role in completing missing information by relying on our memories of past experiences. It is through these associated experiences that we are able to effectively utilize the information gathered by our senses.

Conscious Hearing

With our refined understanding of the hearing process, we can begin to use the sense of hearing as a portal to meditation. For our meditative purposes, we will not rely on the illusory identification system that the brain uses to convey information to us. Instead, we will simply listen to all sound, without any attempt to identify or understand it.

To enhance our listening skills, we will eliminate mental biases and focus on hearing from all directions, despite our ears being less sensitive to sounds above, below, or behind us. By intentionally listening in every direction without trying to identify specific sounds, we can avoid entering a beta wave state that hinders meditation.

Here is how the process of mindful hearing takes place:

Time

Two sessions, each lasting five minutes.

Position

Choose a location where you can sit or stand comfortably without any distractions.

Eyes

Initially, you practice with your eyes closed, but when you practice again, your eyes are open.

Process

Take a moment to set your timer for five minutes. Once ready, gently close your eyes and focus on releasing any tension in your body. As you do so, allow yourself to fully absorb the sounds that surround you, without the need to label or recognize them. Let the experience of sound wash over you, and you will soon find yourself entering a profound state of meditation in under a minute.

When you notice yourself being drawn to or irritated by a particular sound, your analytical, noisy brain hemisphere kicks in, disrupting your meditative state. To stay in a meditative state, just embrace all sounds impartially without trying to label them. However, if there's a sound that could harm your eardrums, take steps to safeguard your ears.

Restart the timer once it expires and begin the meditation again, this time keeping your eyes open. Initially, you may find yourself distracted by the things you see, but simply redirect your focus to the sounds around you. Soon enough, your mind will settle down, and you will experience a profound state of meditation.

"Go within every day and find the inner strength, so that the world cannot blow your candle out" – Katherine Dunham

Conscious Olfaction

The sense of smell, known as olfaction, is frequently underestimated in today's world. However, for hunter-gatherer communities across the globe, it holds immense importance and is integral to their daily activities.

Recent research published in the Journal Science has shed light on the incredible power of the human sense of smell. Surprisingly, the human nose is able to detect over one trillion distinct scents, far surpassing our ability to differentiate between colors (several million) and audible tones (around half a million).

In our modern society, humans have become disconnected from their sense of smell due to the lack of necessity for survival. However, recent research has revealed that we possess a far greater olfactory capacity than we are aware of, and the impact of scents on our bodies is largely unconscious. Despite lacking the vocabulary to describe the countless scents our noses can detect; our bodies still react to them on various levels.

The sense of smell plays a crucial role as a chemical detection sense, enabling the identification of minute molecules in the environment. What's fascinating is that this ability is not limited to complex organisms alone but is also found in single-celled organisms. In the case of land mammals, such as humans, the sense of smell operates in a distinctive manner.

Molecules suspended in the atmosphere settle within the nasal mucus and dissolve. Beneath the mucus layer, specialized receptor cells, known as neurons, perceive the scent. These neurons convey the information through electrical signals to the posterior part of the nasal cavity, specifically to the olfactory bulb, which is essentially an extension of the brain. Subsequently, the signals are directly transmitted to the limbic system, impacting emotions and memory, as well as to the neocortex, influencing conscious thought.

Have you ever taken notice of how specific aromas can trigger vivid recollections of individuals, locations, and experiences from long ago, even from your early childhood? This connection is established because your sense of smell acts as a direct conduit between your memory and emotional center and the world around you.

The chemicals that come into contact with your nose effectively engage some of the most advanced and ancient structures in your brain, which are closely tied to emotions, memories, motivations, and automatic behaviors that largely operate beneath your conscious mind.

A fascinating study published in the journal Psychological Science highlights the fact that humans can actually detect the smells associated with fear and disgust. What's even more intriguing is that when we encounter these scents, our brain subconsciously reacts by registering the same emotions, which can be observed through our facial expressions. This research indicates that scents possess a contagious element (de Groot et al.).

Studies indicate that women typically possess a more acute sense of smell than men, while younger individuals generally exhibit a stronger sense of smell than older individuals. The prevailing explanation for this trend is that women utilize their sense of smell to identify suitable partners and establish connections with their newborns.

Regardless of whether you are male or female, young or old, the sense of smell has the strongest connection to the unconscious region of our brain that governs memory, emotion, and motivation. Just imagine the transformative impact if we could increase consciousness in this area, leading to more harmonious and constructive memories, emotions, and motivations.

With conscious olfaction, you can effortlessly surpass the boundaries inherent in traditional meditation methods, enabling you to achieve greater heights and more.

The steps involved in conscious olfaction are as follows:

Time

Begin your timer for a duration of fifteen minutes.

Position

You can sit or stand in whatever way feels most comfortable to you.

Eyes

Practice with your eyes shut the first time, and with them open the second time around.

Process

Breathe deeply and consciously, focusing on the sensation of air entering and leaving your body. Pay attention to the air's characteristics like pressure, humidity, and freshness, along with your sense of smell.

Don't focus on pinpointing a specific scent; instead, embrace all smells as you feel the air moving through your nostrils. When you sense the transition to alpha, a state of tranquility and relaxation, open your eyes to resume meditation. What changes did you observe? Did your physical sensations shift? Did you experience relaxation? Did your mind become still?

The act of consciously recognizing smells can greatly contribute to a sense of calmness in most individuals. In general, when we neglect our sense of smell, we quickly lose awareness. However, by intentionally maintaining an awareness of different scents for an extended period, we can experience a heightened state of tranquility and clarity, gradually reducing any habitual tendencies towards anxiety or depression.

The act of smelling can lead to relaxation for your mind and body by consciously stimulating the limbic system, which is the emotional center of the brain. It is important to remember that when you consciously smell, you are deliberately engaging a part of your brain that is typically beyond your conscious awareness.

This means that you have the ability to bring about positive changes in your brain regarding emotions and past traumas. If during this meditation, old negative emotions or mental narratives surface, the most effective approach to reprogramming your brain is to fully embrace the process of conscious olfaction and continue with it until the negativity dissipates. Simply keep consciously smelling.

It is important to note that once you transition to the alpha state, you may notice that you are automatically peripherally aware when you open your eyes. This serves as a clear indication that you are in a conscious alpha state. However, if you are unable to fully perceive your entire visual field upon opening your eyes, it means that you have not yet made the shift to a conscious alpha state.

In such a case, close your eyes again and consciously focus on your sense of smell, bringing your awareness to the nasal passages and lungs as you breathe. Continue this practice until you relax even further, and then try opening your eyes once more. It is highly probable that you will now naturally perceive the complete visual field.

Keep in mind that your mind may try to attribute particular smells to a narrative voice while you meditate. However, this intrusion from the serial processing mind can hinder your progress. Rather than getting caught up in labeling smells or resisting this inclination, calmly acknowledge its occurrence and refocus your awareness on all smells and the sensation of air passing through your nostrils.

It's perfectly fine if you're not able to detect strong scents, as your sense of smell can be impacted by various factors like your physical condition, age, and the environment. The main goal is to tap into the essence of smell, which is essentially a feeling that enhances awareness. So, if you struggle with your sense of smell, try to tune into the sensations in your nostrils and air passages.

Numerous meditation traditions incorporate various breath techniques, often with intricate details. Surprisingly, very few of these traditions emphasize the connection between breathing and the sense of smell. In my opinion, this is a significant oversight, as the sense of smell plays a crucial role in our psychological well-being.

In the present day, people are greatly dependent on using foveal (focused) vision, causing a state of stress and agitation in the mind through cortisol releases in the brain. A person who pays attention to their sense of smell is likely to be a calm and collected individual.

Becoming more attuned to your sense of smell and the act of breathing can be a powerful tool in combating anxiety and depression. You may experience a sense of liberation and relief from negative emotions. In general, after your second practice of conscious olfaction, you should be able to do it effortlessly with your eyes open from the beginning.

> "Whatever is fluid, soft, and yielding will overcome whatever is rigid and hard. What is soft is strong" – Lao Tzu

Conscious Tasting

The sense of taste, similar to the sense of smell, is a chemical detection sense. However, unlike the sense of smell that can detect an extensive range of scents, the sense of taste is commonly believed to distinguish only five flavors – sweet, sour, salty, bitter, and savory. Nevertheless, there are those who contend that pungency (spiciness) and the taste of fat are also perceived.

The sense of taste collaborates closely with the sense of smell in identifying flavors. When we chew food, our tongue not only registers taste but also engages with the texture, providing more input to the brain and influencing our perception of taste. To understand the interplay between taste and smell, try tasting something while blocking your nose – you'll quickly realize how much smell contributes to our ability to taste different flavors.

The sense of taste plays a crucial role in allowing humans to differentiate between foods that are nutritious and those that may be harmful. This process begins with the breakdown of food into basic chemicals by digestive enzymes in saliva. These chemicals are then detected by the taste buds, which are located on the tongue. It is estimated that the tongue contains between 2,000 and 5,000 taste buds.

Additionally, taste buds can also be found in the throat, as well as on the roof, sides, and back of the mouth. Each taste bud consists of 50 to 100 taste receptor cells that send electrical signals to the brain. The brain then processes these signals and creates the perception of taste that we experience.

The ability to taste helps us distinguish between nutrients and toxins. Sweetness usually means energy-rich foods, while bitterness can signal potential poisons. Taste buds can only detect a limited number of flavors, so our sense of taste heavily relies on our sense of smell.

The temperature of the air and food plays a significant role in how we perceive taste. Cold temperatures can hinder our sense of smell, resulting in a less acute sense of taste. On the other hand, warming up food enhances our sense of smell, ultimately improving our ability to taste different flavors. This is why we tend to prefer heated foods over cold ones, and why ice cream may not taste as flavorful when cold.

Remember that taste, much like smell, is sensitive to temperature changes. When meditating, be attentive to the sensations without becoming preoccupied with the specific tastes, as they can differ based on temperature. Focus on the overall experience and the sensations in your tongue and mouth.

The process of conscious taste is as follows:

Time

Set a timer for a 15-minute interval.

Position

Feel free to choose whether to sit or stand, ensuring that you are completely at ease.

Eyes

When you attempt it for the first time, make sure to close your eyes.

Process

Increase your mindfulness of the sensation in your mouth and the general taste sensation.

Take note that you might notice hints of flavors that you had earlier in the day, but refrain from trying to pinpoint exact tastes. Simply be mindful of the sensation of taste and the feeling in your mouth as if it were your very first encounter with it. Pay close attention to when the transition to alpha state takes place.

It's clear that the process is easy to follow, as many individuals can achieve a shift to alpha wave within a minute by simply concentrating on taste and mouth sensations.

> "Nowhere can man find a quieter or more untroubled
> retreat than in his own soul" – Marcus Aurelius

Conscious Feeling

The fundamental aspect of conscious feeling primarily revolves around bodily awareness. This awareness encompasses two key components: proprioception and interoception. Proprioception refers to our ability to sense the body's position in space, acting as an internal map that allows us to know the location of our body parts without relying on visual cues.

On the other hand, interoception relates to our perception of the body's physiological condition. It provides us with valuable information about various sensations, including touch, temperature, muscle activity, pain, tickling, itching, hunger, thirst, the need to yawn or take a breath, sexual arousal, heartbeat, vasomotor activity, and the feeling of fullness in the bladder, stomach, rectum, and esophagus.

Our bodily awareness is influenced by receptors present in our joints, muscles, ligaments, and connective tissues. These receptors provide essential information about the compression and decompression of our joints. This information is transmitted through the spinal cord and reaches the unconscious regions of our brain. As a result, unless you actively make an effort to pay attention to your body, you may remain unaware of your bodily position.

Despite not always being conscious of it, your body is usually capable of keeping you upright and safe during your daily activities. That's why I call it a generally unconscious sense.

By bodily awareness, we do not mean your thoughts or opinions about your physical appearance. Instead, We are referring to the direct sensory awareness of your body's state, sensations, and posture.

This includes the feeling of your body's contact with the environment, such as the sensation of the floor beneath your feet, the chair against your buttocks, the touch of your skin against clothing, the air around you, and so on. It encompasses the complete array of bodily sensations, both internal and external.

Medical and psychological literature describes heightened body awareness as leading to worsening symptoms of anxiety and panic disorders, and to an increase in pain. The reason for this outcome is that the medical and psychological community has defined awareness as being focus. When we focus on physical symptoms, we may ruminate on and experience magnification of symptoms, leading us to states of high anxiety.

The concept of bodily awareness in the medical/psychological field differs significantly from the understanding of awareness among body-mind practitioners. Body-mind practitioners base their awareness on a calm perception, rather than a tense one.

Many practices that integrate the body and mind aim to heighten awareness of the physical self, like tai chi, yoga, Feldenkrais, Alexander technique, and breathwork. Nevertheless, traditional meditation serves as a prime illustration of the serene body-mind approach.

When practicing traditional forms of meditation, the goal is to concentrate on one thing while simultaneously staying relaxed. By employing relaxed concentration in body-mind practices, individuals can access an alpha brainwave state, resulting in favorable medical and psychological outcomes.

Conversely, a stressed or anxious focus on emotions can induce a beta wave state, contributing to heightened anxiety and negative consequences as acknowledged within the medical community.

Extensive research has consistently highlighted the advantages of cultivating a relaxed sense of bodily awareness. These studies strongly suggest that engaging in body-mind practices can potentially alleviate the symptoms of several conditions, such as chronic lower back pain (Mehling et al.), congestive heart failure (Baas et al.), chronic renal failure (Christensen et al.), and irritable bowel syndrome (Eriksson et al.).

The Total Embodiment Method takes awareness to a new level compared to the conventional body-mind approach. Rather than fixating on a particular body part, we cultivate a relaxed awareness of the entire body. Strangely enough, this broadened awareness heightens our sensitivity to subtle bodily cues without inducing anxiety, similar to how we can perceive the subtle blinking of faint stars more distinctly by being attentive to our peripheral vision.

Here is the Total Embodiment Method process of conscious bodily awareness:

Time

Give yourself about a minute between steps. The entire process should not last more than fifteen minutes for your initial experience.

Position

To start with, find a place where you can relax without too many distractions. If you tend to feel drowsy or fall asleep easily while lying down, consider sitting upright or standing instead.

Eyes

To ease ourselves into the practice of bodily awareness, we will begin by dividing the body into sections. However, it is important to note that this sectional approach is temporary. Soon enough, we will transition into practicing full bodily awareness as our default method.

While sitting comfortably, focus on relaxing your entire feet and pay attention to the overall space you are working on, instead of getting fixated on specific points of discomfort or pain. Allow the painful areas to remain in the background of your awareness as you follow the steps below.

Take a moment to vividly connect with the sensations in the area between your ankles and knees, and consciously release any tightness or stress in that region. Shift your focus to the space from your knees to your hips, feeling it deeply and intentionally relaxing that area. When you feel prepared, bring your awareness to the area from your hips to your lower ribcage, embracing its vibrancy and consciously letting go of any tension.

Direct your focus towards the space between your lower ribs and collarbones, and let go of any tension in that area. When you feel prepared to progress, direct your vibrant attention to the area between your collar bones and the top of your head. Take a moment to relax it deeply. Start by becoming aware of the space between your collar bones and your elbows.

Take a moment to intentionally relax that space. Next, shift your attention to the area between your elbows and your wrists. Allow yourself to relax completely. Now, bring your focus to your hands and fingers. Take a moment to relax this area with utmost care. Lastly, pay attention to the entirety of your body, both internally and externally, and relax your entire being, maintaining just enough tension to stand tall.

"The secret of change is to focus all of your energy, not on fighting the old, but on building the new" – Socrates

The Warriors Meditation

The Warrior's Meditation serves as the fundamental level 1 TEM meditation practice. It lays the groundwork for developing a neural foundation that will gradually enable mindfulness to permeate your everyday life. Similar to the accomplished Samurai, who attains profound serenity and clarity amidst the turmoil of combat, with dedicated practice, you too can attain tranquility and clarity in your dynamic daily life.

In order to grasp the concept of the Warrior's Meditation, envision a scenario on a battlefield where a lone Samurai finds himself surrounded by numerous adversaries who are determined to end his life. A beginner's focus constantly shifts from one opponent to another in a state of anxious self-defense.

Eventually, exhaustion sets in and defeat becomes inevitable. On the other hand, a skilled warrior distributes his attention evenly in all directions, yet still experiences unease as he mentally strategizes his next move. If his opponents possess true expertise, his thoughts and anxiety may ultimately lead to his downfall.

In contrast, a master's attention, akin to that of the skilled warrior, is evenly dispersed, but he remains as tranquil as a serene pond. Without dwelling on what actions he should take, his body instinctively responds in accordance with the demands of the present moment.

One might question the similarities between the Samurai's

experiences and contemporary life. In an ideal scenario, there are no armies or assassins attempting to harm you or your community.

In various ways, we, as modern individuals, exhibit similarities to the Samurai. Due to our busy schedules, we are unable to allocate multiple hours daily for meditation. Hence, we require a meditation practice that seamlessly fits into our fast-paced lives. This allows us to carry out our tasks with a deep sense of mindfulness. The purpose of the Warrior's Meditation is to help you communicate from a place of profound awareness.

The act of reading can easily trap a newcomer to the TEM process in beta wave. Therefore, I recommend familiarizing yourself with the meditation steps before attempting the Warrior's Meditation. This will allow you to understand the process and perform the meditation without the need to read. Once you have grasped the steps, put the book down and give it a shot.

It should be emphasized that our approach to meditation involves utilizing the senses as a means of guidance. Should any of the five fundamental senses be lacking, there is no cause for alarm, as the brain will make up for their absence. For example, if one is unable to hear, while concentrating on the auditory sense, they can redirect their attention to the physical sensations in their ears. By doing so, they can attain the same depth of meditation as an individual with all five senses.

Time

In general, the initial encounter with the Warrior's Meditation typically lasts for approximately 15 to 20 minutes. The duration may differ for each individual as it is crucial to navigate through the process based on personal sensations. Once you become accustomed to the steps and have engaged in the Warrior's Meditation a few times, it is advisable to set a timer for a preferred duration. This allows you to focus solely on your dedicated practice sessions without the need to be concerned about time.

Position

Aim for comfort, but refrain from lying down initially to avoid feeling drowsy and falling asleep. Establishing a link between meditation and sleep may lead to difficulties in maintaining focus and alertness throughout your meditation practice.

Eyes

Open for basic practice.

Process

Start the Warrior's Meditation by performing a series of vagal breaths, which will swiftly induce relaxation in both the body and mind.

Take a deep breath and allow it to expand your lungs in a manner that is truly pleasurable. Adjust the pressure of the stretch by engaging your abdomen, spine, shoulders, and neck. Focus on creating a wonderful feeling. Exhale slowly and repeat the sequence.

After achieving a state of calmness and clarity in both your body and mind, proceed to the subsequent stage of the meditation.

Direct your gaze forward, encompassing the entire visual field. If needed, utilize your outstretched arms to locate the outer limits of your peripheral vision when transitioning from focused vision.

To locate the peripheral edge, focus straight ahead and extend your arms out to the sides without shifting your gaze. Move your hands back until they are out of sight, then wiggle your fingers. Gradually bring your hands forward until the wiggling is just visible in your peripheral vision. While maintaining the wiggling fingers at the edge of your visual field, move them in a clockwise circular motion to identify the complete outer edge of your peripheral vision.

In terms of our peripheral vision, you will notice that the upper and lower limits are relatively narrow, spanning roughly 90 degrees vertically. However, the horizontal range is much wider, providing us with approximately 180 degrees of visibility. Once you have identified the entire outer edge of your peripheral field of vision, it is recommended to relax your arms.

To ensure a comfortable meditation experience, take a few minutes to relax and focus on your peripheral vision to acclimate to it and allow your perception to expand before advancing to the next stage. After becoming accustomed and relaxed in the awareness of the entire visual field, proceed to the next step.

Acquire a comprehensive awareness of the entire range of audible sensations by allowing all sounds to permeate your body without fixating on or attempting to identify any specific sound. By setting aside our biases, preferences, and aversions, we will discover that we can engage in this meditation practice even in a noisy environment, as every sound becomes permissible.

However, it is always prudent to safeguard our ears from excessively loud sounds in order to protect their well-being. Dedicate a few minutes to applying a vibrant state of consciousness to all sounds, whether they are nearby or distant. Once you have achieved a state of relaxed and conscious listening, proceed to the next stage.

Develop an awareness of the sense of smell and the sensation of air moving through the nostrils into the lungs. While you may detect various scents around you, including those of your own body and the food you consumed earlier, refrain from trying to label them.

Simply observe the array of smells without getting fixated on any one in particular. If you find yourself unable to perceive any odors, there is no need to worry, as pinpointing specific scents is not the goal. Instead, approach the experience with an open and impartial mindset, free from preoccupation with specifics. Relax and savor the moment.

Center your awareness on the sense of taste and the sensations in your mouth. You may become aware of flavors lingering from earlier meals, but resist the urge to identify them. Simply enjoy delving into the overall taste experience and the various mouth sensations like warmth, moisture, hardness, softness, and more. Striking a balance between relaxation and active engagement is key here. Allow yourself a brief period to adjust to the taste sensation before progressing to the subsequent step in the meditation, which focuses on bodily awareness.

Attain a deep awareness of the entire external surface of your body, as well as the internal sensations, as though you were perceiving them for the very first time. While there may be instances of discomfort or pain, exercise caution not to solely focus on those specific areas. Instead, allow your consciousness to encompass the entirety of your body simultaneously. Take a brief period to unwind and fully embrace this state of heightened bodily awareness.

Lastly, permit your meditative state to transcend the confines of your body and encompass the space around you in a spherical fashion. Imagine it as though the very core of your existence is released to perceive the expanse that exists beyond the boundaries of your physical self.

Many individuals may feel tempted to exert immense internal pressure during this phase, hoping to inflate themselves like a balloon. However, this approach contradicts our goal of attaining a calm and mindful state that can enhance our everyday experiences. Rather than forcing ourselves, we should embrace this process as a source of pleasure and liberation.

In the confines of a room, it is common for our intentions and emotions to unconsciously fixate on the physical boundaries. However, this inclination to halt at surfaces reflects a restrictive belief, as intentions have the capacity to transcend these limitations.

Surfaces hold no sway over our intentions, so it is essential to allow our intentions and emotions to extend beyond the walls, ceiling, and floor. Throughout your meditation, maintain an unwavering awareness, with the aim of gradually reducing your focus. Embrace a state of relaxation and relish in the richness of your existence.

The Warrior's Meditation at this stage offers numerous advantages, one of which is the enhancement of our functional attentiveness to the entire space surrounding us. This has a profound impact on the brain, leading to its transformation and enabling a greater contextual awareness of the external world and a deeper understanding of the internal psyche.

> "Meditation is not spacing-out or running away. In fact, it is being totally honest with ourselves" – Kathleen McDonald

Rising from the Warrior's Meditation

The objective of the Warrior's Meditation is not to remain still, even though it can be utilized for profound, stationary meditation. The main aim is to integrate situational awareness into our dynamic everyday routines.

It is important not to link standing up or walking with the conclusion of meditation, as is common in various other meditation practices. Rather, we should uphold a lively spatial awareness as we transition to a standing posture, move around, and engage in our daily activities.

By and large, the practice of the Warrior's Meditation usually does not result in a drastic reduction in blood pressure that would lead to potential fainting when standing up. Nevertheless, it is recommended to raise blood pressure slightly before standing as a safety measure. This can also be utilized as an opportunity to enhance the ability to stay in a meditative state while increasing blood pressure.

To effectively raise your blood pressure, it is crucial to maintain a constant awareness of your surroundings while performing the necessary movements. A helpful analogy to understand this concept is to think of the windows on your computer screen. Just like you can have one window in the foreground and another in the background, we will prioritize spatial awareness while allowing the stimulating movement to remain in the background of your consciousness.

By incorporating this approach into your meditation, the movement will seamlessly blend in without disrupting your focus. To achieve this, shift your body weight from side to side, forward and backward, and gently wiggle your fingers and toes. These simple movements should effectively elevate your blood pressure to safe levels before you transition to a standing position.

Now that you are up, strive to sustain spatial awareness as you navigate through your day.

Summary of the Warrior's Meditation

1. Engage in a series of vagal breaths to induce relaxation in both the body and mind.

2. Focus on the entirety of your visual field.

3. Be mindful of all sounds, whether they are close by or in the distance.

4. Acknowledge your sense of smell and the sensations in your breathing passages.

5. Be aware of your sense of taste and the sensations in your mouth.

6. Recognize the sensations throughout your entire body.

7. Extend your awareness beyond your body, encompassing the space surrounding you.

8. Gradually rise, maintaining a primary focus on spatial awareness, wiggle your fingers and toes, and gently sway from side to side to ensure your blood pressure is stable before standing. Stand mindfully.

In Conclusion

If we start feeling a bit overwhelmed by the sensory experience during the Warrior's Meditation, it could be a sign that we are exerting too much effort with our senses. The most frequent issue is with our eyes, which tend to unconsciously bulge as we try to perceive the peripheral field.

To address this, we should aim to relax our eyes and allow them to naturally observe the peripheral field without any strain. Additionally, it is beneficial to relax our shoulders, as they often accumulate unconscious tension.

One of the usual ways we strain our bodies during meditation is by attempting to grasp onto all our senses simultaneously. To address this, we should smoothly transition from one sense to the next, for example, from sight to sound to smell, and simply relax and have confidence that our previous senses will provide us with the necessary information without the need to concentrate on all senses at once.

Regular meditation practice has the potential to cultivate a sense of expanding awareness, bolstering the psychological resilience of meditators and diminishing their reactivity to stressors and perceived personal affronts.

By meditating, individuals can perceive themselves in a non-personal manner, fostering objectivity and insight that can aid in breaking free from unhealthy emotional patterns. This depersonalizing impact gradually protects against negative traits like pettiness, selfishness, neuroses, and narcissism. As you become less responsive to unworthy distractions, you'll likely experience a reduction in wasted time and energy.

Through the practice of the Warrior's Meditation, individuals may observe a sense of awakening in their bodies. This awakening enables the body to react autonomously to avoid potential threats or to move towards advantageous paths. Personally, I let my body take the lead in my writing process.

It feels as though the words are flowing through me, rather than me actively writing them. I am confident that musicians and athletes may also experience moments of complete absorption in their craft. This state of complete absorption is commonly known as being "in the zone."

Regardless of the meditative technique mentioned earlier, meditation is indispensable for any spiritual journey. It plays a crucial role in awakening Kundalini energy and is also imperative for men who wish to retain their semen.

> "Untrained warriors are soon killed on the battlefield;
> so also persons untrained in the art of preserving their
> inner peace are quickly riddled by the bullets of worry and
> restlessness in active life" – Paramahansa Yogananda

Biblioghraphy:

The Warrior's Meditation by Richard L. Haight

www.theserpentsway.com

TAKE CARE OF YOUR
S O U L

"My soul is my guide, for my soul is of that abode. I will not speak of the earthly. I am of the UNKNOWN."

[You are the soul, the body and the mind in one]

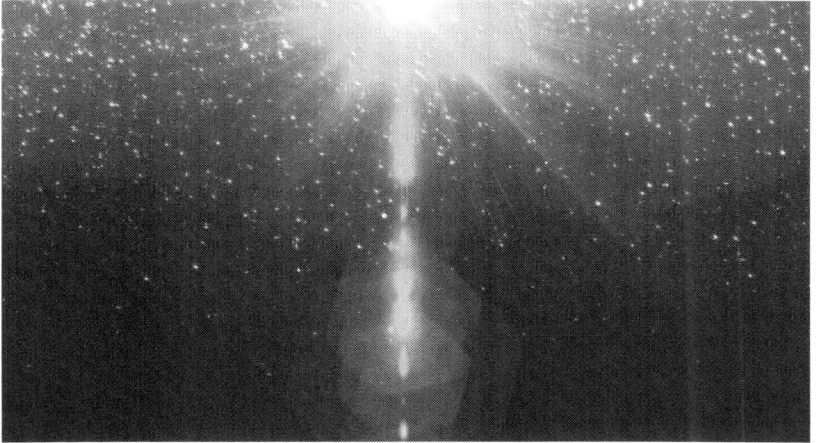

14

SAINT GERMAIN ON CREATING

WHEN THE GREAT ALCHEMIST'S (*the true Creator of everything*) Spirit breathed into man's nostrils the breath of life, the fire of creative Spirit filled the clay tabernacle. An embryonic god was born. The practical aspects of alchemy are to be found in manifestation only in the one who has developed the power to execute the design of freedom. Whatsoever bindeth is not the friend of the alchemist; yet it is the goal of the alchemist to bind the soul to its immortal tryst in order that the pact of life might be sanctified even as the precious gift of individual identity is accepted.

Now, the identity of the alchemist is to be found in the mandate "create!" What we say we become; we create with our words which derive from our little mind where the source of it is the Great Source itself. In order that the alchemist might obey, the fiery energies of creation are dispensed to him each moment. Like crystal beads descending upon a crystal thread, the energies of the creative essence of life descend into the chalice of consciousness.

Neither halting nor delaying in their appointed course, they continue into the repository of man's being. Here they create a build up for good or for ill as each iota of universal energy passes through the recording nexus and is imprinted with the fiat of creation. The fiat reflects the intent of the will of the individual monad. When the fiat is withheld, there is an idling of the great comic furnace as the talent of the descending chaliced moment is rejected by the consciousness and becomes an opportunity lost. When there is no qualification, no fiat of intent, the energy retains only the God-identification of the talent without the stamp of individualization; and thus, it falls into the coffers of the lifestream's record without having received so much as an erg of qualification.

The creative process, then, is of little significance to the individual who does not recognize the mandate to create, for by his nonrecognition he forfeits his God-given prerogative. As a result of man's neglect of his responsibility, the fiat of God was given that is recorded in the Book of Revelation: "Thou art neither cold not hot: I would thou wert cold or hot. So then because thou art lukewarm, and neither cold nor hot, I will spue thee out of my mouth."

The fiat to create must be heeded, but let us pray God that men heed well the sovereign responsibility that Life has given them to create after the pattern of the divine seed. Well might they emulate the elder gods of the race and the royal priesthood of the order of Melchizedek in their creative endeavors, that they might convey upon the energy chain of life that peculiar and fascinating aspect of cosmic genius that is the nature of the eternal God. So long as individuals allow themselves to be kept in a state of constant fear, so long as they deny themselves the great benefits of universal hope, so long as they fail to take into account the meaning of the promise "His mercy endureth forever," so long shall they continue in ignorance to deny themselves the bliss that exudes from the rightful exercise of spiritual privilege.

To belittle the soul of man, to cast it down into a sense of sin, frustration, and self-condemnation is the work of the princes of darkness. But it is ever the forte of the sons of heaven, of the Ascended Masters, and of the cosmic beings to elevate that supreme nobility which is both the fabric and the content of the soul into such prominence in the life of man that he might hear the dominant word of the eternal God in ringing tones, "Thou art my Son; this day have I begotten thee."

Man must enter into a pact of universal trust based on his own inner commitment to the grace of God that will not prohibit him from exercising the power of the living Word to emulate the Masters, to emulate the Only Begotten of the Father, to emulate the Spirit of comfort and truth. And when he does, he will find opening to his consciousness a new method of cleansing his soul by the power of the LORD'S Spirit. Then he will come to understand the meaning of the statement made concerning Abraham of old that Abraham's faith "was imputed unto him for righteousness: and he was called the Friend of God." And so it is "not by might, nor by power, but by my Spirit, saith the LORD of hosts, that man accomplishes the alchemical feat of transmuting the base metals of human consciousness into the gold of Christed Illumination.

"Human might and human power can never change man's darkness into light, nor can they deliver humanity from the sense of struggle that bans from their lives the acknowledgement of the God-given potential that lies within the domain of the self." From the book *Saint Germain On Alchemy* by Mark L. Prophet

The victorious accomplishments of the Master Jesus, together with the "greater works" which he promised that the disciples of Christ would do "because I go unto my Father," remain in this age. as in ages past, a fiat of universal freedom. Thus, the works of the alchemists of the Spirit beckon the souls of men to forsake their attitudes of self-condemnation, self-pity, self-denegation, self-indulgence, and overreaction to the errors of the past. For when men learn to forgive and forget their own mistakes, their hearts will rejoice in the acceptance of the word from on high "What God hath cleansed, that call not though common."

Recognizing, then, that the potential of every man rests in his immersion in the great soundless-sound stream of living light-energy from the heart of the Universal Christ, we say: Let the power of the Holy Spirit, worlds without end, exert its mighty cosmic pressures upon the soul of the would-be alchemist until he emerges from the fiery furnace pliable, whited, and pure in the willingness to obey the fiat of the Lord to create first a clean heart and then to renew in self a right spirit. God is Spirit; and as the Supreme Alchemist who has the power to work change in the Universe, he is able to convey his passion for freedom to the soul of any man who will accept it. His is the passion which produces in man the miracle of unfoldment through a sense of the real. His is the passion that will drive from the temple those money changers and bargainers who would literally *sell the souls of men in the marketplaces of the world.*

*sell the souls of men in the marketplaces of the world.

Your birth certificate has value in the worldwide stock exchange. The money changers and bargainers are the unjust controllers (including the mega corporations) that make billions and trillions of dollars every year by selling people's birth certificate value. That money belongs to the people and not to a small group of heartless greedy ones that created the fraud Birth Certificate a.k.a. the STRAWAN fictional 2D character that enslaved the souls of men (and women and children). To read about the STRAWMAN subject on how they enslaved the whole world through the illusion called "legal documents" read the book *You are not a STRAWAN you are the ZYGOTE* by Saimir X. Kercanaj.

We are concerned with creating in the student of alchemy a conscious awareness of the power of the Spirit to convey the transmutative effect of the Universal Alchemist into the lives and beings of embodied humanity. It is through this awareness that they shall be exalted in a manner which they have never before experienced, for at least they shall have recognized that within themselves the cosmic key-seed of universal potential lies literally entombed.

> "To resurrect, then, the Spirit of the Cosmic Alchemist means that we must seek before we shall find, that we must knock before the door shall be opened."

We must, in the ritual of true faith, be content to commit ourselves to him who is able to keep and to save to the uttermost those who believe in his manifold purposes. These are centralized in the one purpose of unfolding the consciousness of the stone which the builders have rejected, of the Christ that is the head of every man. In the concept of the abundant life is to be found the radio-active principle of the expanding God consciousness into which any man may drink without depriving his brother of one iota of his inheritance.

There is no need, then, for jealousy or a sense of struggle to function in the lives of the true alchemist; and wise are they who will submit themselves to the pressures of the divine law, who will seek to purge themselves of all unclean habits stemming from mortal density and of doubt and fear, which are the root cause of man's nonfulfillment of his destiny. It is incumbent upon each life, then, to create according to the patterns made in the havens. He who can produce the miracle of these patterns in his life is also able to have all things added unto him; for by his seeking first the kingdom of heaven, the earth herself yields to his dominion.

In these series on intermediate alchemy, I am, in the name of Almighty God, creating in the consciousness of the disciples who apply themselves to this study a spirit of inner communion. Through this spirit - a focus of my own flame - the Most High God and the hierarchy of Light shall focus, by the power of universal Love, a climate within the consciousness of the student that shall enable him to obtain his rightful place in the divine scheme. Then the kingdom will flower and men will perceive that they need not engage in struggle or seek by violent means to obtain that which God is ever ready to give unto them. The lingering fear in the worlds of men is of the dark, whereas faith, hope, and charity are the great triune bearers of light who exalt 'Reality' and lead men toward the light. Ready for action, I remain the Knight Commander, Saint Germain

Bibliography

SAINT GERMAIN ON ALCHEMY by Mark L. Prophet and Elizabeth Clare Prophet

15

THE NEED FOR HEALING – MESSAGES FROM THE ARCTURIANS

HEALING IS VERY IMPORTANT to you now as you go through the transition of releasing attachments. You are releasing some of the early life history that you have had on the planet, even though you continue to maintain an interaction with those past energies. The key to healing lies in interacting with those energies, including both past-life energy and energy from childhood wounds. The energies should become fluid. They are part of your history and being. The experiences you have had on the planET are all relevant. You are seeking a unity, an integration of all of those energies. They will remain a part of your new integration. Once you understand them, you will be able to interact with the energies and they will not dominate you. You will then become unstuck.

We are following many of you all of the time. We connect with you directly when you call on us. When you do not call on us, we do not intervene or interfere in any way with your ongoing life patterns. We will only work with you if you ask us to, and out interaction is not in interference with your karma. We will give you information and be receptive to you when you call on us. We are able to see all of your life patterns. We can see where you are going, what is going to develop, and how your physical bodies are going to unfold. We are very keyed in to your health. You can call on us in particular to assist you in your health developments. We study how you respond to physical diseases and other physical problems. We are aware of your physical limitations. We are also aware that you will be able to transcend those limitations when you go into the higher realms. It is important for your own development that you learn to work within your limitations on the physical plane. However, you are all able to overcome many of the physical problems you are currently experiencing. One aspect of our mission is to assist you in healing. We do healings through a method which we ask you to etherically project yourselves through a corridor and up to our ships so that we can work with you. Your health problems can be a nuisance at times, as you already know. Some of you have particularly complex health problems, yet they do not have to hinder you in your evolvement toward the goal of higher consciousness and interdimensional work. This is very important for you to understand.

We are aware of the difficulty in your immune systems that many are experiencing. Some of you already sense the compromise of your immune system. It is a challenge for you to remain in a state of health on this planet. This is again why we ask you to join us in the corridors where we are able you clear much of the densities and much of the negative energy that attaches to you. New Arcturian ships have arrived in your sector of your solar system from the Arcturian area. We have brought special lightships, special healing energy, and special healers with us, to assist those of you who ask for our assistance. We are serious about wanting to assist you, and we know that the most direct way is through healing. We have the technology, and we have the mental and spiritual ability to work directly with you.

"We also specialize in soul regeneration. There are souls who, because of their darkness, because of their evilness and density, appear to be in a state of total annihilation. Some have speculated that these souls have been wiped out. However, we have been working on soul regeneration, including the souls of evil leaders. Souls can be regenerated through special assistance and work. It is important for those who engage in soul regeneration to be highly focused, and maintain close contact with their group soul energy. We have worked with whole groups and even with entire planets that have been annihilated through atomic weaponry or nuclear disasters. They were much in need of soul generation."

HEALING ON THE ARCTURIAN SHIPS
Our healing methods have to do with aligning your frequencies and clearing all your bodies. We provide a direct connection with you by

providing an interdimensional corridor, and by bringing our ships in a space over your physical presence. We send down a beam of light to help you become cleansed, feel lighter, and get in touch with yourself. We can raise your etheric self, and bring that part of you to our ship. On board, we use a healing library and healing chambers to activate and recharge your energy. You can also reconnect to earlier times and other soul lives when you are with us. If you want to be healed in our ships, you must practice thought projection. *You must be able to project yourself to the ships through thought*. This is an important aspect. We use a highly advanced technique of **meridian therapy** on the ships. Rather than using pins and needles, we use our thoughts to center certain energy waves.

You are connecting to us now by reading these words. We can also give you sounds that you can work with in your meditations. We prefer to work with you in a chamber. We ask you to thought-project yourselves into the chamber, and then we can take you and the chamber up very nicely. You might conceive of the chamber as a kind of exotic phone booth.

It has a circular top, and you can put a chair in it or whatever you wish. You can perhaps conceive of it as even having stained glass windows. **We would like you to use the sound of our name, the Arcturian, to align with us**.

Some of you have had experiences on our ships, but they have not been as intense as you would have liked them to be. It requires a conscious commitment on your part to allow us to work with you. We prefer to work with you in a conscious state.

You can start with a conscious request for healing, and then go to sleep, as opposed to being taken to a healing chamber during a deep sleep.

We find we are able to work with you more effectively when you consciously make the commitment of your own free will. We are then able to accomplish more. We have special healing centers that use sound waves to work with the energy of your organs. Much of our healing is related to organ energy and organ problems. It is our healing specialty. We ask you now to raise your spirit energy, come into an interdimensional corridor directly above your head, and enter the area of or ship that we call the **blue room.** The blue room is reserved for healing and rejuvenation. We have set aside chairs in the chambers for you. You receive an intense charge of blue light, and a loving spirit energy flows through you now. It is magnificently warm and loving. It activates energy for you. We have been taught by the Andromedans how to activate the blue light. We put more and more blue light into your auric field. It is very powerful – a blue healing energy, a telepathic form of energy.

Continue to sit in the blue room and look out at the wall in front of you. We have provided you a view of the galaxy. You can also see the different colors of the star Arcturus, which is very close now. You are looking out a special window so that you do not have to experience any harmful effects of the rays from Arcturus. This is a very powerful method of activation. Identify the star that you wish to connect with, and then the energy you need with come to you. **Know that your crown chakra is now being flooded with blue light, the light of the spiritual insight**. It is anchored within you. This blue light ranges from a light blue to a deep blue. It contains the light and the deep blue colors together. In these colors, the deep blue does not do away with the light blue. You never erase an octave; you just add to it.

The earth vibration on the third dimension is a slower vibration. Your higher energies are steadily depleted by the third-dimensional Earth process. We know the slower vibration of the earth and how it draws your energy. Thus, need to recharge as often as you can. You will need to have many doses of this blue light in the blue chamber. You will want to continue to come back to this healing chamber. If you return to the blue healing chambers, you will eventually be able to hold a higher octave of the blue light. This is part of what you need to do for ascension – gain a higher octave that you can stabilize. It is necessary even for us to return to the blue healing chambers in order to maintain our frequency.

PERSONAL CLEARINGS

Many of you still do not recall your commitment and your instructions before you came into the third dimension on earth. However, it is true that you volunteered for this mission and that deep in your heart, want to be of assistance and service in the highest possible way. Many of you are working very hard on your own personal clearings. This has to do with resolving your karma and personal problems. It also involves opening up your chakras and your energy field to receive and interact with fifth-dimensional energy. It is a great challenge for many of you to balance your personal problems and the resolution of those problems with helping others and service to Earth. We wish to speak to all who are experiencing personal difficulties. We are concerned about your personal problems. We are sympathetic to your situation, and we have compassion for you. We know that there are not a high percentage of light workers on this planet. Each of you is incredibly valuable. When you are clearer and more resolved with your personal problems, then you will be a better transmitter of this fifth-dimensional energy.

We are going to give you guidelines to assist you in clearing any energy that may be hampering you.

First, open your heart chakra wider.

Second, connect an energy link between your third eye and your heart.

Third, mentally project a date in the future when you wish to see a complete resolution of the difficulty. This can be thirty days, fifty days, and so on.

Fourth, create a pathway of light from the present moment to that date that you have chosen.

Fifth, when you reach that date with the pathway of light, create a resolution to your problem in your mind and project it at that point.

Sixth, from that date in your projection, send an energy beam to an Arcturian ship that is in the Jupiter corridor in your solar system. By sending that beam, you give us permission to send energy into your pathway to assist you.

Seventh, receive from us the connection from our ship to you, and this completes the energy path.

Eighth, keep that energy flowing!

In many cases, your problems can be resolved by such a heightened energy and heightened perspective. **When you connect your heart with your third eye, you are also able to terminate the karma that is involved in the problem you have**.

That moves you more quickly to a resolution. You do not need to be burdened any further. Most of the problems that you have can be resolved in a six-week period. We know that might sound phenomenal, but there are very few problems that we have seen with lightworkers that are not resolvable within six weeks. Clearly we cannot interfere in your karma. However, in the method that we have just described, you are in charge. You are asking us to bring an energy to you that will assist you. This is not interference. We are simply working together by your request.

TACHYON ENERGY
Tachyon energy is a pulsing energy very similar to the basic energy

force of the universe. You will find the same pulsing motion in the human heart and in the auric field. The tachyon energy used in our galaxy is a force that some have compared to the universal chi energy. Tachyon healing focuses on utilizing chi, the life force. Chi energy can be placed in stones and other articles and then transmitted into cellular structures, such as the human body.

Holding tachyon energy in rocks is similar to the energy retainment found in crystals. You can transmit your thought patterns into the crystal, which holds the thoughts as mental energy transmission. Crystals must be cleared to remove negative thought patterns. When working with tachyon energy, however, there is no need to clear the stone, since tachyon articles sustain and generate chi energy. And unlike crystals, tachyon stones do not require programming.

Tachyon energy fulfills a need unmet by crystals for the transmutation of healing life force energy. This life force energy can help star-seeds and healers by providing a greater unity and balance for those open to the ascension process. The tachyon stones can accelerate your spiritual work by increasing the vibratory rate of your mental and auric fields. As you resonate with the tachyon pulse, your rate of vibration increases. Then in meditation, you will be able to duplicate that higher vibration by yourself. The goal is to use tachyon energy to help you access deeper states of consciousness. Eventually, you will be able to access these states without tachyon stones.

The sources of tachyon energy are actually outside your solar system. The energy is coming in through cosmic forces-through comets and so forth. "Tachyon" refers to the star of the same name, which is known to many galactic travelers. The source of this energy is believed to originate from that star system. The information about tachyon energy and the technology for its use are extremely important and useful for you now. You will need to learn several methods, including the tachyon method, for accelerating your process. What we are saying now is very important: All of you will find it necessary to accelerate your energy field. **When you are not accelerating, when you are physically or mentally stuck in some way, that is a sign that you need to have an acceleration**. Do not be afraid to accelerate. What might be most useful is to accelerate your connections as well – that is, accelerate your contacts with your guides and extraterrestrial beings. Simply put, many of you will get stuck in lower energy patterns. It will be very difficult to get out without assistance, so do not hesitate to use the contacts you have with us.

SOUND AND COLOR

The sound of the name tachyon is very powerful. You can increase the power of the tachyon energy by speaking the word itself, which will help release the power of the stones. Tachyon is a galactic word, similar to the Hebrew word *Zohar*, or the brilliance. Sound enhances tachyon healing. It is useful to play certain music during healing, including computer-generated sounds. The music helps both the healer and the receiver to resonate with the pulse. Once you both are in resonance with the tachyon pulse, then powerful healing can take effect. It can be described as a settling in. In order to get the full benefit of the tachyon treatment, you must be open to it, and resonate with the pulse.

There are various levels of sound vibrations that can be used to accelerate the healing. For example, using a slow rhythmic sound will help you to enter a trance state. As you become more comfortable, the speed of the rhythms can be increased. The receiver's vibration will increase as the rhythm of sounds increases in speed. To give you an idea of the effects of sound, we will help the channel reproduce useful sounds when doing a tachyon treatment. [Chants]: "tac...tac." Various levels and speeds of sound vibrations can be used. For example, using that sound slowly will help the person you are healing slow his or her pulse. First, have the person adjust to the energy field by listening to a slow-paced sound. Then you can raise the speed of the sound to help the person increase his or her vibration. Tachyons energies used this way will raise the person's overall vibration, which will be very healing.

We want to speak very briefly about the use of color with tachyon energy. Colors that can be especially useful are in the range of the magentas, the reds, the blues, and the purples. The effects of tachyon energy can be accelerated by the proper use of colors. We recommend that when you work with people seeking tachyon treatment, you set up a room with special lights. Also, be sensitive to the colors in the room. For example, it would be helpful to use a special sheet or blanket of the colors mentioned above. The colors that the healer wears can also be important as part of the integrative approach of a tachyon energy treatment. The more you are aware of harmonizing all environmental aspects, the more powerful the tachyon treatment will be.

Tachyon energy can be used to enhance meditation. The stones can accelerate thought patterns of universal healing through the life force energy. An actual cellular reawakening can occur after a tachyon treatment. Tachyon energy can also affect eyesight in a positive way. Corrective work can be done with tachyon stones, especially when done in conjunction with color therapy.

TACHYON HEALING SESSIONS

Tachyon items, when placed around your body, help you to resonate with the pulsation and harmonious flow of the stones. Tachyon healing works by helping you to resonate with the stone's pulsation. Your vibratory fields and your auric fields will be enhanced. The acceleration from the tachyon energy, however, can be overpowering. That is why we want you to be careful to monitor it. In the beginning, we recommend short periods of treatment so that the person can build up to the tachyon energy. A beginning treatment may be 12 to 14 minutes long, combined with a polarity balancing, alignment, or gentle massage afterwards. As you work with a person over a period of time, he or she may be to tolerate 28 minutes. Treatment time goes up in sevens. Thus, you can go from fourteen to twenty-one to twenty-eight minutes. It is important to stick to the factor of seven in determining the length of the treatment. We do not recommend that you go beyond the twenty-eight-minute limit unless there is a specific purpose for lengthening the treatment. Most will find twenty-eight minutes more than sufficient.

We also recommend a twenty-eight-minute balance afterward. If you work for someone for fourteen-minutes of tachyon treatment, then we recommend a fourteen-minute period afterward for energy balancing using non-touching techniques. Do not physically touch the person until after the fourteen-minute balance period. The reason for this is that the person's energy field is still in a state of flux. The energy is still sensitive, and you must respect this sensitivity. We recommend that the person receiving the treatment continue to follow his own pulse in meditation after the tachyon stones are removed. This will help to continue the healing effects and will enhance the balancing.

To stimulate just one area without an overall balancing can be productive, but it will not have as long-lasting an effect as using an integrated approach. It is better to have a treatment with the stones in which there is balancing and an integration of the energy. That ensures that the whole system is put in balance. If you have a problem and treat that area alone, the original unbalance that manifested could switch to another area later. We prefer that the tachyon work be done by a healer who can use a more integrative approach. When the healer works with the person in an integrated way, then effective treatment can occur by leaving the tachyon energy near the body for longer periods. If the healer uses the tachyon energy alone, without a corresponding balancing, then longer tachyon healing will not be as beneficial. The body should not get too used to tachyon energy. Because it is such a powerful energy, it is important to maintain the body's sensitivity to it. Compare the tachyon treatment to a drug that is used daily. A drug tolerance is easily built up, and then it is not as effective. The dosage has to be increased in order to obtain the same effect. Similarly, a tolerance can be built to the tachyon treatments as well. It is best to delegate its use, in separate periods with mental balancing, concentrated awareness of the pulsation, and an attempt to integrate and harmonize with the energy.

In the book *Self-Empowerment* by Saimir Kercanaj, the author has this to say about the Med Beds, the spiritual healing chambers...

*Med beds are benevolent A.I. (artificial intelligence) controlled plasma and **tachyon energy healing pods**. Another name for med beds is 'Tachyon energy celestial chambers.' The term med-bed may not be how they will finally be called as it has been capitalized by others that make products which are not representative of the original. So, This technology is a 6th dimensional spiritual technology. This technology accesses hidden DNA memory to re-atomize the body for optimal health and longevity. How does this technology works? You lie on the device (super advanced bed). You will be placed in deep sleep. Any artificial devices like knees, hips, pacemaker, tooth fillings will be atomized and replaced with the healthy original. Which means it will grow, for example a missing limb. You think that is impossible? Think again.*

A salamander can regenerate any amputated limbs. Why would the Creator give these abilities to only certain animals? The truth is that we all have this ability. No, it is not science fiction. Something is considered science fiction or impossible because of a lack of innerstanding. Let me make you an example that I already made in one of my other books. Before the phones were invented, what would you if someone said that we will eventually operate a device that you can voice and video chat with anyone in the world instantly? You would think that's nonsense. Is it nonsense now? Of course not. Advancement is accomplished from dreamers, from curious people, from those that strive to go beyond the norm.

In the case of the med beds, it is a technology invented on a higher dimension. A dimension where only love exists. Have in mind that the 6th dimension is the last dimension where physicality exists. From the 7th dimension and up, only energy/spirit lives. These celestial chambers (healing med-beds) will not just be brought down to 3d. We must raise our vibration higher than where we are. Technically we are not anymore on the 3rd dimension. That ended in 1987 when the convergence happened. We are on the transitioning period. Worldwide consciousness dictates whether med-beds become a reality in our world, for the masses of course. After you are done in this med-bed, your limbs, assuming you were missing any will be as you never lost them.

Any diseases will be gone. Say "bye bye" to gray hair, period, pimples, freckles, or anything else that you may want to get rid of. It is my belief (I can discard my belief with any new information that will contradict my beliefs) that this is possible. My belief (actually knowingness)*is based on reflecting my inner knowing about our powerful abilities given by the Creator. The reason why we should raise our vibration is so that our DNA also gets upgraded. No matter how healthy you may be eating or drinking, if you have negative thoughts and feelings, you will still be tied in a 2 stranded DNA reality/state of existence.*

Technically, the Celestial Chambers are already here, you just can't see them. Your eyes only see in 3d dimension for now. The more you raise your frequency, the more things that you wouldn't normally see, you will notice. These chambers will be used to shift from 3d reality into a 5d reality. The crystal chamber will be used to shift your physical 3-D body into 5-D light being.

Just so you do not get confused and think that other dimensions are somewhere out there.

All dimensions are where you are right now. You just have to tune to whichever dimension you feel it's your home, a dimension of love or that of hate. Think of dimensions like radio channels. The radio is the whole creation, in this case, Earth. The people, animals etc. are the sounds (music) that come from the radio channels playing. People's actions determine if life is wonderful (beautiful music) or suffering/ struggling (aweful low frequency music).

BUILDING AN ENERGY COCOON

Humans, as galactic beings, are highly intelligent beings. We know that you do not believe how intelligent you are because of the many emotional problems that are on the planet and the many emotional problems that you have all experienced personally.

This (the above paragraph) is not a criticism. It's simply an observation. Your emotional bodies on the Earth are very underdeveloped. We wonder at times how you are able to keep yourself in balance at all; your emotional bodies are constantly being submitted to deviant electromagnetic energy that is bombarding your planet from human-made sources. It is the deviant electromagnetic radiation that is coming from your nuclear bombs that are being tested.

The deviant electromagnetic energy comes from the high-frequency and low-frequency radio sources that your government is experimenting with, and deviant electromagnetic waves created by so many of the airplanes that are flying overhead. We could go on and on. Fortunately, you are such resilient beings. For the most part, you are able to adapt. But it would be highly beneficial to create a cocoon of energy around yourselves for your own protection.

The cocoon of energy will provide stability around your electromagnetic fields. Your cocoon energy needs to be strengthened so that you will not experience auric fractures. This is what is happening now. When auric fractures occur, you can experience deviant electromagnetic energies that can create discomfort. You have heard that an energy cocoon can also be called a protective bubble of white light. What is important is that this white light, or cocoon, can be sensitive enough to block electromagnetic radiation and some of the other energy sources that you do not want to experience. Auric fractures can occur from distorted electromagnetic energy. These fractures can trigger what you have called the déjà vu experience.

We will give you instructions on how to create this cocoon around you because it is going to be vital for all of you to learn how to protect yourselves. You need to do this for many reasons. The most prominent reason is that you must keep your mental balance. We could not travel through the many different zones that we do or travel within the galactic sphere unless we were able to control ourselves mentally and energetically.

Most extraterrestrial beings will not come into physical manifestation because they do not want to expose themselves to the lower electromagnetic vibrations. This is going to be one of the biggest problems in your culture when finally realize the dangers that you are exposing yourselves and your children to from distorted electromagnetic vibrations. It is everywhere on the planet now, and to come onto this planet and into this manifestation requires high levels of protection from the cocoon.

To create the **COCOON**, we ask that you start with a star tetrahedron (Star of David) approximately 3-4 feet (90-120cm) above your head. From that star, bring twelve lines down in a sloping fashion, continuing until they reach below your body around your feet. You must do that for each vertical line. Then make a cross line that will move horizontally around your body so that you now have lines intersecting at ninety-degree angles. Build five of those horizontal lines on one side and five on the other side crisscrossing each other. At that point you will have twelve intersecting grid lines. It is very important that you establish *t w e l v e* grid lines. Then you will be able to access our energy field as well as be centered in the energy field that you have created. Once you are in the energy field you have just created, you can sound our expression. [Make a fast, repeating sound]: "**tac, tac, tac.**" This sound will clear out all extraneous electromagnetic energy that is coming to you. Now put a layer of white light around your cocoon, and then a layer of blue light, and finish with a layer of silver light. Now your cocoon is complete. We hope you have been trying to do this as you read these words. You will now be in a state of protection, and you can bring yourself into a state of balance where you have harmonized and stabilized your own electromagnetic vibrations.

BRINGING BACK GALACTIC IMAGES

For those who have built their cocoons, you can be beamed up into an area on our ship in a dimensional holding pattern. You can come into our ships and rest peacefully. You can move into a special room we have for you, a room of silver-blue healing light. Your intellectual capabilities are manifested through the brain. The spirit force that guides your brain is an electromagnetic vibrational energy. You are cleansed and sharpened as this silver-blue light comes into the part of your soul that manifests your mental intelligence.

Still on our ship, we spin the whole room you are in, in a tight, fast circle and heightened centrifugal force. Feel the room continue to spin, continue to increase in vibration, and continue to go round faster, faster and faster. Look out of the room that we are in on the ship and see the stars that are before you, the stars of the Arcturian system. Feel the starlight from those blue stars that you can see. Know that for some, this is your home system, and we have been patiently waiting for you to return. Do not worry about the time frame because we are not in Earth time. It is not a problem of patience as you may think of it from your linear perspective.

See the stars and the Arcturian stargate, and see the image of those coming into the stargate that is protected by the Arcturians. As these higher-consciousness beings enter the stargate from one side, they also leave going through the stargate, leaving in pure spirit, in pure galactic form. It is a spiritual graduation. As you begin to access our energy, we ask you to bring back some of these galactic images into reality so that others can see them. Sharing these images will activate others to remember their source. This is such an important exercise because so many of you are struggling with your self-image. It has been shattered by so many forces impacting your emotional body and severely distorted by the negative implants that are constantly coming to you. The goal, however, is not to completely remember who you are, because it will throw you off balance if you have not fully accomplished the clearing process. Focus on clarity, on the stability of the mental process, and the remembering will occur. Some will remember differently than others. That is because some have a different perspective. Do not be confused by those having different memories. Go with your own soul memory.

Gently rock yourselves around, and spin yourselves down from our ship into a place where you can re-enter your own consciousness in your physical body. Spin yourself down. Your bodies are happy to receive your spirits. Your mind has been charged, cleansed, cleared and activated.

Channeled by David K. Miller

TAMO's note: This cocoon is so powerful. If you are not that capable of visualizing the whole process, then we suggest you draw or paint, or play a musical instrument or anything creative that catapults you away and outside from the comfortable cell/prison. We are creative beings; we can imagine and manifest everything we wish. Exercise your creative powers. If for example you are working as an accountant, then you are stuck in a left-brain mentality. The left-brain hemisphere is responsible for logic, numbers, statistics etc. We suggest you become creative on your daily routine so that both of your brain hemisphere balance in harmony.

Even if you haven't managed to connect with the Arcturians yet and entering in one of their ships, when you create the cocoon, if you feel like goosebumps or any other happy/beautiful sensation, then that is a sign that you internal intelligence is activating. It means that you are connecting with your true self which the source of it is the Creation itself. Anything you want to master; you must practice regularly. Just as you can easily run because you practiced by walking, similarly you will be able to easily activate your Light Body Vehicle/ Cocoon or Merkaba. It is easier said than done when you don't believe in yourself but it is easier done than said when you know and practice your powerful abilities that you possess. Discipline is the ultimate tool that is needed to achieve anything you desire, provided that what you desire will contribute to the betterment of the world and not the destruction of it.

Bibliography

Connecting With The Arcturians by David K. Miller

Self Empowerment: BOOK ONE by Saimir Kercanaj

16

EGO/SATAN/DEATH – SOUL/GOD/ LIFE, WHICH ONES WILL YOU FEED?

THROUGHOUT TIME, FOR THOUSANDS OF YEARS, people have used these two terms, God and Satan. These are simply states of existence, states of perception of which ever reality you create at any given moment. Only he who doesn't know himself will thank or blame external entities, ideologies for their fortune or their misfortune. It is easy to blame God or Satan when things don't go as you plan. Your thoughts and words are the building blocks of anything that you materialize in your life. Every moment of the day, you are the sole responsible person for however your life goes. Life happens now. If you wander in the past and in the future, the present will flee away. **"God"** means good, or your higher self. **"Satan"** mean bad or your lower self. You are both Satan and God at the same time. That's why you were given a brain for, to create your own paradise or hell, you were given a free will to do whatever you wish to do, but there are consequences if you don't operate in accordance with the natural law which means that you must not harm another person, must not lie or deceive. Must not be greedy etc. If you do those things, sooner or later it will come back to you, that's what karma means, 'action'. For any action or inaction, there is an equal reaction. The more you feed something with your thoughts, the more possibility for you to manifest the end result of your thoughts, desires or intentions. The material world that we live in, is transient and impermanent.

Anything physical, no matter who firmly we grasp it, can be taken away from us because they're all temporary. We are not temporary, we are eternal. Our spirit of course, the physical body is but a temporary flesh and bones garment.

> "He who through the error of attachment loves his body, abides wandering in darkness, sensible and suffering the things of death, but he who realizes that the body is but the tomb of his soul, rises to immortality." - HERMES

Your higher self does not judge, compare, or demand that you defeat or be better than anyone. Don't let anyone define who you are. Discover your own identity and let your presence reveal your true self. Until the ego evolves to become one with your true self, you will remain a slave to your own ego. Being ego driven in your life is living in a dumbed down reality of the real thing as opposed to being soul driven. Egotistical people are the major gossipers.

Remember that rumors are carried by haters, spread by fools and accepted by idiots. Distance yourself from fools that spend their time gossiping. A spiritual awakening is not usually pleasant. It often feels like confusion, frustration, anger, sadness, or being out of place. A spiritual awakening can be uncomfortable and challenging because it is an intense time of personal growth. Despite how difficult it may feel, you are not going crazy, you are evolving. You are considered crazy only to those that haven't gone through the awakening process yet.

> "To the occultist, birth is death and death is an awakening. The mystics of ancient days taught that to be born into the physical world was to enter a tomb, for no other plane of nature is so unresponsive, so limited as the earth-world." – Manly P. Hall

Your soul has reincarnated many times. Here are some signs :

You see through illusions very easily.
You are an extremely sensitive person.
You have a very strong intuition.
You may feel like you don't belong here (but you do- it is difficult for a reason because the soul growth received in this dimension is massive). You crave a deep connection and deep conversations with people who are good for you.
You have a high level of respect for nature, animals, other humans and everything in nature. Things like talents and gifts come to you easily because you have practiced them in other lifetimes. You tend to

require a lot of time alone to recharge. Don't fall for your ego driven desires.

When you are aligned with egoistical vibrations, you will tend to think that you are sinning while you could be in the process of entering the right path. Recognize the duality of yin/yang-soul/ego. Adam and Eve are allegories for the yin/yang principles within you. The journey is to balance these energies. The forbidden fruit was the orgasm (and the carnism).

The gateway to Eden is through congregation of sexual alchemy. This is known as the great Arcanum, the secret teachings of tantra hidden within all religions. Learn to love your Light half, your Dark half, and the shades of gray in between so you can have a balanced whole being. Be yourself wherever you are. Don't agree to things to keep the peace. That's a trauma response. When you do this, you are disrespecting your boundaries. Be decisive and say to yourself, "No more making myself uncomfortable for others to feel comfortable". You have the ability to control yourself. You can run your life instead of running it down. Be balanced.

Do good and if you mistakenly do bad then it's important that you recognize the deed and improve next time. Don't think of it as a sin if you were to do something that would be seen as a negative from society. There is no such a thing as sin. People do good and bad things. Sin is a myth. The concept of sin was created as a recruitment method to get people to join an immoral religious organization and to extort money from them. Religious leaders and believers tell you that you have an imaginary problem and coincidentally, they have a magic cure for your imaginary problem. When you align with your higher self, you won't fall for your ego's tricks. Work on your shadow self. Your shadow self is a part of you that carries all of your traumas and negative patterns accumulated throughout your life. It is the part of you that you try to keep hidden from the world and from yourself.

> "Unless you learn to face your own shadows, you will continue to see them in others, because the world outside of you is only a reflection of the world inside you".

Little do you realize that connecting to and embracing your shadow becomes a very crucial step in the healing process. You have to be able to admit that you have (we all do) negative patterns of thinking and behaving before you can heal them. Once you can admit this, your awareness of your own behavior will become much more apparent and you will be able to objectively see where you are stuck and messing up. Shadow work is the epitome of true accountability. Unless you do the shadow work, you will always be confused and not know how and why the things that happen in your life happen the way they do.

You are here to innerstand yourself, your purpose and not to be innerstood. Nobody can innerstand you because only you can know you and that is through the shadow work. Which one will you feed, the Ego or the Soul? When Ego dies, the Soul awakens. Technically, the Ego is part of you, it never dies, it can only be tamed. Ego knows that its life is short that's why it causes us to steal, be greedy and many other detrimental actions that have been troublesome for society for a long time. Since Ego sees life as lacking, it entices us to become greedy. How do you tame this? By appreciating what you have, instead of wanting more than what you need. In this case you tame Ego, but be careful that it can crawl back in your life like a parasite so you must be self aware and conscious of every choice/action you make. It is easy to stray off the path, especially when you spend too much time listening to other people's opinion rather than listening to you inner voice. Even what I'm writing here is an opinion from your point of view.

Regardless of who says what, in the end it is you that decides what to do with any information. After all you have free will, don't you think? But if you believe that you don't have free will, then you are still right, you are the creator of your own reality, a reality that will be repeated over and over again until you choose to be the leader of your life, until you realize that you are the director of this movie called life.

> "The problem is that we have allowed our egos, the part
> of us that is separate from God and separate from each
> other, to dominate our lives." – Wayne Dyer

One of the fundamental pillars of most spiritual practices revolves around a distinction between different levels of self. Depending on the practice, this might be presented in terms of levels of consciousness, or as your ability to embody higher ideals, or higher versions of yourself. Or, perhaps most commonly, the idea is often talked about in terms of separating the ego from the soul. In the spiritual sense, your ego is the person you normally think of as "you." The ego has physical needs, wants, and desires, while the soul exists on a higher non-physical plane.

Often, we think of the soul as guiding the ego forward in it's level of awareness, a sort of "Higher Self" that can inspire you and point you in the right direction. How do you separate the soul from the ego? How do you know when the thoughts you're thinking are "inspired" from a higher level, or if they are just another layer of the ego's thoughts? How can you identify which thoughts come from the Spirit, and which are from Self? And how can you use this difference to **follow your intuition** and live a more inspired and fulfilled life?

In spiritual terms, you can think of your ego as the "everyday you" who lives and works in the world.

Your ego is the driver of your everyday needs, which includes your biggest accomplishments, dreams and aspirations, as well as the things you perceive as faults or wrongdoings. In other words, the ego is the little voice in your head, constantly thinking thoughts about your life.

The ego:

-Tells you what you "should" or "must" do.
-Analyzes whether life is going to plan.
-Critiques you when things could be better.
-Complains about the world around you.
-Judges yourself and others for their actions.
-Drives most of your daily emotions.

What is the Purpose of Ego?

It is common for spiritual seekers to frame the ego in a negative light. On the surface, it seems like the ego blocks us from achieving higher levels of consciousness, but this is not negative.

The purpose of the ego is to define the singularity of your individual experience. It provides contrast, which encourages your inner growth.

"The problem arises when the inner self, or Atman, is not fully awake. In this weakened state, instead of knowing our true status as unlimited, non-local pure consciousness, our sense of identity becomes

overshadowed by our external experience. This is object referral instead of self-referral. Our sense of "I" is then defined by our body, our relationships, our possessions, our fears and desires. This unawakened version of the ego does generate distractions and obstacles to spiritual growth just by virtue of this self-perpetuating object referral pattern. The ego in itself is not the villain. Once self-realization occurs, the ego's misappropriation of identity dissolves and its simple function of providing individuality to experience enlightenment will remain." – Deepak Chopra

Thus, the problem is not that we have an ego. The problem is that – for most of us – the ego drives most of our thoughts and actions, without us ever becoming aware of it. It runs wild, and we must learn **how to tame the ego** if we want to live more meaningful, spiritual lives. Or else, an untamed ego simply means spiritual death, it means to just exist as opposed to live our lives to the fullest.

Bibliography

I Am The Key That Opens All Doors by Saimir Kercanaj

www.thejoywithin.org

Sexual Alchemy
KUNDALINI

"When you succeed in awakening the Kundalini, so that it starts to move out of its mere potentiality, you necessarily start a world which is totally different from our world. It is the world of eternity."

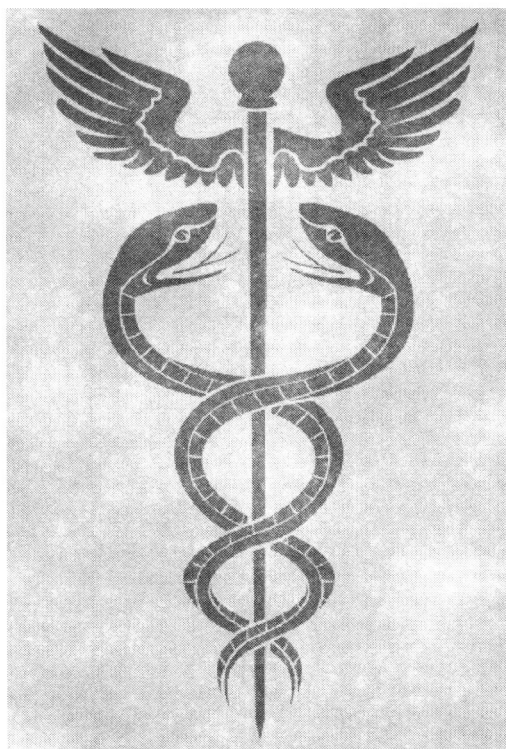

17

MASTURBATION & DEGENERATION

"Wastage of semen brings nervous weakness, exhaustion, and premature death. Sexual acts destroy the vigor of your mind, body and indriyas and annihilates memory, understanding, and the intellect. Semen is a dynamic force. It should be converted into spiritual energy with pure thoughts and meditation. Those who are very eager to have God-realization should observe unbroken celibacy." - Swami Sivananda

CREATION IS SEXUAL ENERGY. The sexual energy is the most powerful force in the universe. It is an immense power that if you don't know how to control/manipulate it, you can destroy yourself and others. Because it is such a powerful force and because most people don't know how to properly control it, the dark magicians/ wizards use people's ignorance against themselves (using our own ignorance against us) where people continue to remain ignorant and powerless. How do they use it against people? One word – PORN.

Porn breeds lust, destruction in relationships and families, porn weakens a human, it robs of his/her life force. In this chapter you should truly understand the root cause of all problems and the consequences of wasting the sexual energy or the vital force. To awaken the kundalini, we must first begin to understand the root of the problem. You can water the leaves of the tree all you want, if the root of the problem needs attention, all your efforts will go to waste if you don't fix what immediately needs fixing.

BLACK MAGIC

The chosen image above represents degeneration through their gloomy, dark, and depressive nature. This selection serves a dual purpose: firstly, it accurately portrays the decline of reproductive energy, with masturbation and orgasm being viewed as forms of degeneration and decay. Secondly, the images also serve as symbols of black magic, reflecting the ritualistic nature of pornography as a form of dark magic.

On the "Shadow Dragon" page/tab (at **www.theserpentsway.com**), it was mentioned by Thoth, an Atlantean Priest-King, that upon establishing a province in ancient Egypt following the sinking of Atlantis, he declared that individuals were resorting to black magic in order to acquire power and wealth.

In addition, we discussed Manly P. Hall's explanation of ceremonial magic in ancient times. He distinguished between White Magic, which is used for the benefit of others, and Black Magic, which is focused on self-serving purposes. Hall suggested that the positive aspects of White Magic from ancient ceremonial practices deteriorated into corruption and distortion due to the influence of Black Magic.

It is clear that a logical mind can deduce that following the fall of Atlantis, the use of black magic persisted. In ancient Egypt, black magic took over the spiritual leadership and eventually became the dominant force in the state religion.

This state religion of black magicians incapacitated the intellectual and spiritual growth of the Egyptian citizens. As we learned, the Pharaohs' became a marionette controlled by the Scarlet Council. This council of dark arch-sorcerers was raised to power by the corrupted priesthood.

The current state of humanity is a result of the negative impact of black magic practices from ancient civilizations like Atlantis and Egypt. These practices have led to a degenerated and highly controlled condition that has persisted through the ages.

In the present day, politicians and national governments are mere pawns, carrying out the desires of a hidden and influential power structure that operates in secrecy. The Ancient Scarlet Council of Egypt can be seen as comparable to what is commonly referred to as the 'Deep State' or the term 'Shadow Government'.

Since we referred to national governments and this sinister power structure, Matthew Lacroix, in his book THE ILLUSION OF US: THE SUPPRESSION AND EVOLUTION OF HUMAN CONSCIOUSNESS stated the following:

This concept of nationalism that has been stoked in our society for thousands of years has led to LUST, gluttony, severe poverty, and instability across the planet.

This structure is reinforced by the intense promotion of competition which begins when we are only children. Whether it is with sports, business, or even societal status, humanity is engineered into a constant state of survival against one another.

Instead of a friendly collaboration of ideas with peers, students are pitted against one another in a barbaric population who is dominated by ego and greed for themselves. This toxic viewpoint has turned social interactions into a ceaseless barrage of insults and attacks, as we continuously compete for everything.

There has been a deliberate suppression of consciousness for all developed countries and instability and war in virtually all the rest. To achieve this state of consciousness with an awakened Kundalini, chakras, and all human spiritual abilities activated requires first-and-foremost the preservation of sexual energy.

The deliberate suppression of humanity's spiritual potential by these black sorcerers has been ongoing since the fall of Atlantis. Throughout various civilizations, we can extensively discuss the actions and impact of these sorcerers, even encompassing the disintegration of the contemporary power structure.

Prior to unlocking the door to The World Health Organization, it is essential to confront a significant misconception. Presently, the general population associates the term Occult with malevolence. The exploration of the Occult can actually contribute to the spiritual advancement of humanity.

Occultism according to Will Keller, is the study of the hidden Laws of Nature, specifically those laws which are at work in the visible/mental/spiritual domain far more than those at work in the visible/physical world.

Therefore, Occultism involves the acceptance of a much wider worldview than that which is ordinarily taken by the everyday person. Occultists, then, may be defined as those who study ALL the Laws of Nature, both those are readily seen, and those which are much more difficult to see with the eyes or measuring instruments alone. Let's move along to some more detrimental misinformation and lies that have caused many to be deceived.

> **"The ultimate tyranny in a society is not control by martial law, but control by the psychological manipulation of consciousness, through which reality is defined so that those who exist within it, do not even realize they are in prison"** - *Barbara Marciniak*

18

THE WORLD HEALTH (DISEASE) ORGANIZATION

BY NOW, YOU MAY BE WONDERING how masturbation relates to the content of this (check **Masturbation-Degeneration** at our website https://theserpentsway.com/) article. However, as we progress further, we will connect all the dots. It is important to acknowledge the intellect and strategic approach employed by these dark sorcerers. They possess a profound understanding of the immense power that lies within sexual energy.

The key to human spiritual evolution lies in harnessing sexual energy. Since ancient times, there has been a deliberate agenda to prevent individuals from unlocking their spiritual potential. This suppression is aimed at maintaining control over humanity by keeping them in a state of degeneration.

As with other world organizations born from the ruins of the war of 1940-45 (*the World Trade Organization, International Monetary*

Fund, The World Bank, and The United Nations) The World Health Organization is a transnational superministry, in the case of health.

Beneath the façade of these so-called global institutions lie individuals who, under the guise of humanitarian organizations, are actually black sorcerers. Their sole purpose in creating these entities was to advance an agenda of enslavement, a plan that traces its roots back to the ancient city of Babylon.

The World Health Organization's influence trumps that of its national counterparts, operating without regard for democratic electoral processes. These organizations are undeniably totalitarian in essence.

These organizations hold authority over all national governments. Unfortunately, both these global institutions and national governments have succumbed to corruption. The agenda of the black sorcerers, which these global bodies represent, aims to establish a totalitarian regime of digital control over humanity, reminiscent of a fascist/communist Orwellian society. It is crucial to verify the information I provide by conducting your own research.

According to *PreventGenocide2030.org*, the standing director-general of the World Health Organization is a man named Tedros Adhanom Ghebreyesus. Tedros, as he is frequently called, was elected to the position of director-general on May 23, 2017, becoming the first WHO director-general in history to not be a medical doctor.

Instead of having been a medical doctor, Tedros served ministerial positions for Ethiopia under the regime of the Tigray Peoples' Liberation Front (TPLF), a prolifically violent Marxist organization of which he was a prominent (top three, per the Ethiopian Registrar member of the politburo.

TPLF is currently designated a terrorist organization by the Ethiopian government, and was designated a Tier III terrorist organization by the US Department of Homeland Security on the basis of its violent quest to become the main party of the ruling coalition of Ethiopia, a position it held on to with an iron fist for the better part of three decades.

The US has issued a statement lamenting TPLF's post-reign violence as well. After holding regional and state positions in the early 2000s, Tedros was promoted to Minister of Health of Ethiopia by Prime Minister and chairman of the TPLF, Meles Zenawi, in October of 2005.

During his tenure as health minister, the government referred to Cholera as "acute watery diarrhea", preventing the country from receiving international medical resources, potentially protecting tourism and/or other sources of revenue dear to party leadership.

Since a cholera outbreak in 2006 in the Oromia region, Ethiopia has referred to the disease as "acute watery diarrhea" (AWD), essentially a symptom of the deadly waterborne cholera, which is caused by the Vibrio cholerae bacterium.

Tests at the time by the United Nations confirmed that it was actually cholera." Responsiveness was severely limited by the government's refusal to declare a Cholera epidemic on multiple occasions, and many Ethiopians became sick and succumbed to the disease.

TPLF's manifesto labelled the Amharas, one of the two largest ethnic groups in Ethiopia, the enemy of the Tigray people. Their history of participating in genocide against the Amhara people is well-documented.

According to the Amhara Professionals Union, Tedros appears to share the inclination of the party of which he was third most important member of the standing committee of the Polit bureau.

The organization released a lengthy research document, which will be touched on briefly, as it is too extensive to detail in full here, although readers are encouraged to review it in full on their own time.

The Amhara Professionals Union further accused Tedros of being responsible for a de facto "chemical genocide" during his tenure on account of presiding over "poorly treated and handled chemical waste" in the region.

While this accusation of a secretive depopulation agenda under the guise of family planning and/or poor waste-handling may seem outlandish to sheltered readers, it is far more humane and less incredible than the other more brazen methods of achieving the same end that appear to have been carried out in the region.

As reported to Genocide Watch, the means of ethnic cleansing that have been perpetrated on the Amhara are often of a spectacularly gruesome character.

The APU's treatise also references an audit report from the Global Health Fund's Office of the Inspector General stating, "Dr. Ghebreyesus frequently mentions his role as Chair for Global Fund to fight AIDS, Tuberculosis and Malaria from 2009-2011 but instead of being proud he should rather have been ashamed given the mismanagement of the fund and poor accounting found during his tenure as Minister of FMOH.

Global Fund to Fight AIDS, Tuberculosis and Malaria granted Ethiopia $1,306,035,989 over the years. However, according to the 2012 audit report of the Global Fund's Office of the Inspector General, the office led by Dr. Ghebreyesus and other partner organizations actually inappropriately used the money generously donated by tax payers and requested the Ethiopian government to refund $7,026,929.00.

The inappropriate actions include misappropriation of funds and use of donor funds for unsound programs most of which were used for political purpose, substandard quality of constructed health facilities suggesting Dr. Ghebreyesus government plays with numbers not with quality and ineligible expenditures.

The report stated over $5.5 million was advanced by HAPCO to the FMOH and was still outstanding by February 2011 although the grant expired in August 2010. Overall, the organization led by Dr. Ghebreyesus was noted to have weakness in accounting, poor budget preparation and monitoring, inadequacies of internal audit and overall poor financial management."

Late in 2012, Tedros became Minister of Foreign Affairs, operating with the same level of integrity as he had as Health Minister. A subset of the highlights follow.

Early in his tenure at the position, Saudi Arabia sought to repatriate foreign workers in response to unemployment of native Saudis. Nearly a million Bangladeshis, Indians, Filipinos, Nepalis, Pakistanis and Yemenis are estimated to have left the country.

The Ethiopian government failed to respond, despite a deadline extension. When violence broke out against the Ethiopians in Saudi Arabia, the Ethiopian government didn't bother to respond until Ethiopians started to protest peacefully outside the Saudi embassy in Ethiopia's capital, at which point protesters were promptly beaten and arrested.

"Whilst thousands of its nationals are detained, beaten, killed and raped, the Ethiopian government hangs its negligent head in silence in Addis Ababa, does not act to protect or swiftly repatriate their nationals, and criminalises those protesting in Addis Ababa against the Saudi actions."

In 2014, Tedros personally orchestrated the kidnapping of Andargachew Tsege, as well as reportedly north of 760 additional dissidents by colluding with Yemeni leaders. Then when civil war broke out in Yemen, the Ethiopian prime minister unsurprisingly publicly backed the Yemeni government leaving the hundreds of thousands of Ethiopians in the country an acutely dangerous situation.

When South Africans began killing foreigners on 11 April 2015, including victims from Ethiopia, Mozambique, Bangladesh, and Zimbabwe, other notable African nations sprang into action, with Malawi and Kenya evacuating their citizens Zimbabwe dispatching police and Nigeria issuing a 48-hour ultimatum threatening to shut down their South African operating businesses all within a week of the violence. For his part, Tedros put out a self-and-party-aggrandizing Facebook post.

On April 20th, in lieu of any real response from the Ethiopian government, the Global Alliance for the Rights of Ethiopians, which had formed in response to the government's lack of response to the Saudi situation under Tedros put out a statement both acknowledging that the "grim socio-economic and political situation in Ethiopia is driving thousands of young girls and boys from their home land and exposing them to inhuman treatment abroad" and pleading that the government "take responsibility and take appropriate and immediate action to protect the rights of its citizens".

In November, when Ethiopians were again attacked in South Africa, resulting in half a dozen Ethiopian being murdered in particularly brutal fashion, the response was similarly apathetic. Aboye said the Ethiopian embassy has not given enough help. "We see our brothers getting killed, doused with a three-liter jerrican of kerosene, and no one is helping us when this happens," he said. "We haven't seen anyone sticking up for Ethiopian citizens here."

After a number of Christian Ethiopians were famously beheaded or shot by ISIL extremists in Libya, the government facilitated a rally at the nation's capitol. First decrying what it presents as the government's original repressive response toward the families of the victims, E-Veracity summed up the event's conclusion succinctly, "As it always does, the government started attacking Ethiopians."

Then at the Ireecha Cultural Festival of 2016, the government did some more of what "it always does", attacking and firing into the crowd. Tedros went on record to state "Indeed, it is quite clear from the videos that there was no shooting and the police were unarmed" despite that the video provided by Human Rights Watch showed precisely the opposite.

In 2017, Forbes put out an article showing that though the TPLF-led government received close to $30 billion since coming to power, the same amount, roughly $30 billion, was stolen by TPLF-led government officials.

Its author was David Steinman, a Nobel Peace Prize-nominated economist who directly advised Ethiopia's democracy movement for nearly three decades until it finally broke free of the shackles of the TPLF-led government regime in 2018.

Having a uniquely qualified understanding of the situation among westerners, Steinman lodged a complaint with the International Criminal Court in Hague calling for Tedros to be prosecuted for genocide.

Per British publications, The Times and the Daily Mail, Steinman stated that Tedros "was a crucial decision maker in relation to security service actions that included killing, arbitrarily detaining and torturing Ethiopians" and that the WHO chief oversaw the "killing, and causing serious bodily and mental harm to, members of the Amhara, Konos, Oromo and Somali tribes with intent to destroy those tribes in whole or in part" along with "intimidation of opposition candidates and supporters", including "arbitrary arrest . . . and lengthy pre-trial detention".

This is only a partial resume of the storied pre-WHO career of Tedros Adhanom Ghebreyesus. Sure, it's odd that the same Health Minister leading the only country in the horn of Africa not to have cholera was also the Foreign minister of what was routinely the only country uninterested in repatriating its distressed citizens, and sure kidnapping dissidents and lying about events with publicly available video footage looks bad.

And sure, providing disproportionately high levels of healthcare for your native region for virtually every indicator except for injectable contraceptives used in unprecedented abundance for the ethnic group your party has appeared to be hellbent on genociding since its inception looks suspicious, but have you seen this face?

Clearly, when it came to the brutal crimes and methods of Tedros's party, including those perpetrated under the divisions of the government he was head of, he should have been told—only then could he have truly known!

Of course, if he didn't know the methods used by his own regime, that would imply that he was a half-witted lackey who mindlessly did the bidding of whoever pulled the levers of power.

This presents the uncomfortable binary whereby he was either a genocidal thug, or a half-witted lackey somehow unwittingly complicit in brutality, and one would think in neither circumstance would it make any sense to put this non-medical-doctor at the helm of something like the World Health Organization.

In fact, to anyone with any neural activity at all it appears unmistakable that the only reason to hire Tedros for anything would be in the event that one planned on grotesquely trampling ethical and/or legal standards and needed a lieutenant who could be relied on for unwavering complicity.

Do you truly trust that the organizations affiliated with the United Nations prioritize the well-being of humanity? Do you have confidence in the World Health Organization's commitment to safeguarding individual health interests? Are you convinced that vaccines and self-pleasure contribute to good health? Do you truly believe that the World Health Organization functions as a health-focused entity? Do you sincerely think that these groups would expose the great power of harnessing your sexual energy?

"Those who understand ejaculation know it grossly exploits every gland and organ. With ejaculation, the internal pressure of life is expelled. Leaving behind sex-obsessed men with just enough life force to hold a newspaper, squeeze food through bowels, and make it to a psychiatrist's couch. With ejaculation of sperm, vitality plummets. The big spender loses stamina, his vision weakens. Hair tumbles from his skull. He grows old before his time" - Mantak Chia

19

MISINFORMATION & LIES

Kenneth Saladin stated simply, *"If you want to destroy any nation without war, make adultery or nudity common in the young generation."* Having said that, let's now examine the agenda set forth by individuals who have been involved in the practice of black magic since the time of Atlantis. Specifically, we will focus on the degenerative sexual propaganda promoted by the World Health Organization.

Comprehensive sexuality education (CSE) as it is called by the World Health Organization gives young people so-called accurate, age-appropriate information about sexuality and their sexual and reproductive health, which is critical for their so-called health and survival.

While CSE programmes will be different everywhere, the United Nations' technical guidance – which was developed together by UNESCO, UNFPA, UNICEF, UN Women, UNAIDS and WHO – recommends that these programmes should be based on an established curriculum; scientifically accurate; tailored for different ages; and comprehensive, meaning they cover a range of topics on sexuality and sexual and reproductive health, throughout childhood and adolescence.

Topics covered by CSE, which can also be called so-called life skills, family life education and a variety of other names, include, but are not limited to, families and relationships; respect, consent and bodily autonomy; anatomy, puberty and menstruation; contraception and pregnancy; and sexually transmitted infections, including HIV.

Sexuality education equips children and young people with the knowledge, skills, attitudes and values that help them to protect their health, develop respectful social and sexual relationships, make responsible choices and understand and protect the rights of others.

Evidence consistently shows that high-quality sexuality education delivers positive health outcomes, with lifelong impacts. Young people are more likely to delay the onset of sexual activity – and when they do have sex, to practice safer sex – when they are better informed about their sexuality, sexual health and their rights.

> The World Health Organization doesn't prioritize your rights and health; they are merely a front for black sorcery. If they truly cared, they wouldn't be pushing chemical poison like vaccines during the orchestrated COVID scam. Once you truly tap into the power of harnessing your sexual energy, you'll realize it's the ultimate medicine that can make you immune to all illnesses and diseases.

In an upcoming post, we will delve into the topic of vaccines. Vaccines can have a detrimental impact on the path of Kundalini awakening, but this is intentional. Just like masturbation, vaccines can impede your spiritual progress. Many courageous doctors have already brought attention to the dangers associated with vaccines.

Sexuality education also helps them prepare for and manage physical and emotional changes as they grow up, including during puberty and adolescence, while teaching them about respect, consent and where to go if they need help. This in turn reduces risks from violence, exploitation and abuse.

When should sexuality education begin? According to the World Health Organization, children and adolescents have the right to be educated about themselves and the world around them in any age - and developmentally appropriate manner – and they need this learning for their health and well-being.

Intended to support school-based curricula, the UN's global guidance indicates starting CSE at the age of 5 when formal education typically begins. However, sexuality education is a lifelong process, sometimes beginning earlier, at home, with trusted caregivers. Learning is incremental; what is taught at the earliest ages is very different from what is taught during puberty and adolescence.

With younger learners, teaching about sexuality does not necessarily mean teaching about sex. For instance, for younger age groups, CSE may help children learn about their bodies and to recognize their feelings and emotions, while discussing family life and different types of relationships, decision-making, the basic principles of consent and what to do if violence, bullying or abuse occur. This type of learning establishes the foundation for healthy relationships throughout life.

Does sexuality education encourage masturbation? According to the World Health Organization, CSE does not promote masturbation. However, in our documents, WHO recognizes that children start to explore their bodies through sight and touch at a relatively early age. This is an observation, not a recommendation.

The UN's guidance on sexuality education aims to help countries, practitioners and families provide accurate, up-to-date information related to young people's sexuality, which is appropriate to their stage of development. *This may include correcting misperceptions relating to masturbation such as that it is harmful to health, and – without shaming children – teaching them about their bodies, boundaries and privacy in an age-appropriate way.*

What is the impact of abstinence-based programmes? According to the World Health Organization, there is clear evidence that abstinence-only programmes – which instruct young people to not have sex outside of marriage – are ineffective in preventing early sexual activity and risk-taking behaviour, and potentially harmful to young people's sexual and reproductive health.

CSE therefore addresses safer sex, preparing young people – after careful decision-making – for intimate relationships that may include sexual intercourse or other sexual activity. Evidence shows that such an approach is associated with later onset of sexual activity, reduced practice of risky sexual behaviours (which also helps reduce the incidence of sexually transmitted infections), and increased contraception use.

How can countries use the UN's guidance on sexuality education?

According to the World Health Organization, sexuality education, as with all other issues, WHO provides guidance for policies and programmes based on extensive research evidence and programmatic experience.

The UN global guidance on sexuality education outlines a set of learning objectives beginning at the age of 5. These are intended to be adapted to a country's local context and curriculum. The document itself details how this process of adaptation should occur, including through consultation with experts, parents and young people, alongside research to ensure programmes meet young people's needs.

"Knowledge of the momentary pleasures which can be obtained by sexual indulgences, without the knowledge of their terrible deleterious influence under certain unnatural conditions, is one of the greatest causes of physical weakness, and the pain, unhappiness and disease that accompany this abnormal condition"
- Bernarr A. Macfadden

To control the world's population by weakening them, teach them that masturbation being harmful is nothing but a misperception. The Communist Organization asserts that hindering the spiritual evolution of humanity towards higher consciousness can be achieved by imparting the knowledge **THAT ABSTINENCE-ONLY PROGRAMS ARE INEFFECTIVE** in deterring early sexual activity and risky behavior, and may pose potential harm to the sexual and reproductive health of young individuals.

Numerous search results emerge when conducting a Google search on "Masturbation and Health," showcasing an abundance of information highlighting the purported positive health impacts of this practice. However, such claims are based on misinformation. Throughout history, various ancient philosophies, religions, and mystery schools have long recognized the detrimental consequences associated with squandering one's seed.

In an article titled *10 Benefits of Masturbation*, Men's Health magazine describes for following benefits [actually LIES] of masturbation. The words "LIE" & "TRUE" after each so-called *benefit*, are added by the authors of this book.

1)-It can help lower prostate cancer risk.... **LIE**

2)-It makes you harder.... **LIE**

3) It helps you last longer during sex.... **LIE**

4) It boosts Immunity.... **LIE**

5) It boosts Mood.... **LIE**

6) **It can Help You Fall Asleep**.... TRUE

7) It can Increase Your Life Span.... **LIE**

8) It Can Improve Your Skin.... **LIE**

9) It Helps You To Get to Know Your Body Better....**LIE**

10) It Improves Your Heart Health.... **LIE**

These 10 so-called benefits are all **FALSE** except for number six which should be obvious as to why.

David Wilcock stated in his book FINANCIAL TYRANNY, the following about Media Consolidation. In 1983, there were 50 different independent media companies in the United States. By 2004, this number had reduced to five key players: Time Warner, Disney, News Corporation (FOX), Bertelsmann of Germany and Viacom (formerly CBS).

These five huge corporations - Time, Warner, Disney, Murdoch's News Corporation, Bertelsmann of Germany, and Viacom (formerly CBS) - own most of the newspapers, magazines, books, radio and TV stations, and movie studios of the United States.

These five are not just large - though they are all among the 325 largest corporations in the world - they are unique among all huge corporations: they are a major factor in changing the politics of the United States, and they condition the social values of children and adults alike.

We find ourselves engaged in a battle on two fronts - a spiritual war and an information war. These sources are owned by the dark/ black magicians who are well aware of immense power of sexual energy.

On the contrary, the claim that *an orgasm a day keeps the doctor away* is **absurd** and **false**. For a man, orgasm causes degeneration and decay. It is important to note that the only benefit out of ten is that orgasms can aid in falling asleep, as they deplete your vitality. Engaging in self-pleasure or experiencing orgasm with a partner can have detrimental effects on the body, mind, and spirit.

Throughout our practice, we have delved deep into the teachings of various cultures and traditions to understand the profound effects of semen retention. By immersing ourselves in this knowledge and incorporating it into our daily lives, we have experienced firsthand the transformative power of harnessing sexual energy. Through our journey, we have sought to not only understand the theoretical aspects of this practice but also to embody its principles in our own lives.

Moreover, through our own personal journeys, we have discovered the transformative power of semen retention. By breaking free from the cycle of addiction to porn and masturbation ourselves, we have experienced a profound shift in our physical, emotional, and spiritual well-being. This newfound awareness has enabled us to fully appreciate the importance of preserving and harnessing our sexual energy for personal growth and vitality.

Despite being classified as 100% disabled upon retiring from the military, I have managed to maintain a sense of vitality and youthfulness. This includes feeling mentally, physically, and spiritually akin to someone much younger. However, despite my overall well-being, I have not sought medical attention in the past six years.

After years of enduring the physical strain from military service, particularly the impact on my knees from parachute jumps, I found myself in a state of physical discomfort and exhaustion. The wear and tear on my body had taken a toll, leading me to seek alternative methods to improve my health and well-being. This realization prompted me to explore the practice of semen retention as a means to rejuvenate my body and mind.

Over the years, the wear and tear from weightlifting began to manifest in my body, especially in my elbows, knees, and back. This physical strain served as a constant reminder of the years I dedicated to weight training. Additionally, my struggle with an extreme masturbation addiction took a toll on my body as well. As I entered my late thirties, the consequences of this addiction became more severe, impacting not just my physical health but also my overall well-being.

With the elimination of pain and discomfort through semen retention, I have been able to tap into a wellspring of vitality and energy that has revitalized my body. This surge in strength and resilience has not only transformed my physical well-being but has also empowered me to push my limits in activities like biking, where I now effortlessly tackle lengthy bike rides (25 to 35 miles) multiple times a week.

Since incorporating semen retention into my lifestyle, I have noticed a significant increase in my energy levels and overall productivity. This newfound vigor allows me to hit my home gym regularly throughout the day, maximizing my workouts and seeing better results than ever before.

Despite only getting five hours of sleep each night due to the immense energy levels from retaining, I am amazed by how energized I feel, even as I prepare to rest for the night. This shift in my routine has truly revolutionized my life, allowing me to achieve more and feel better than I ever thought possible.

Consequences of semen loss from masturbation or conventional sex

"Eminent doctors of the west say that various kinds of diseases arise from the loss of semen, particularly in young age. There appear boils on the body, acne or eruptions on the face, blue lines around the eyes, absence of beard, sunken eyes, pale face with anaemia, loss of memory, loss of eye-sightedness, discharge of semen along with urine, enlargement of the testes, pain in the testes, debility, drowsiness, laziness, gloominess, palpitation of the heart, dyspnoea or difficulty in breathing, phthisis, pain in the back, loins, head and joints, weak kidneys, passing urine in sleep, fickle-mindedness, lack of thinking power, bad dreams, wet dreams and restlessness of mind. Mark carefully the evil after-effects that follow the loss of seminal energy! Persons are physically, mentally and morally debilitated by wasting the seminal power on so many occasions for nothing. The body and mind refuse to work energetically. There is a physical and mental lethargy. You experience much exhaustion and weakness." – Swami Sivananda

The addiction has had profound consequences on our well-being. We have personally experienced discomfort in the elbows, knees, and lower back, along with feelings of depression, brain fog, and low self-esteem. Moreover, it has caused a lack of motivation, confidence, and determination. It has also stifled our creativity and stripped away our spiritual abilities. Additionally, it has resulted in a loss of libido, heightened anxiety, and extreme fatigue. Furthermore, it has impacted our ability to concentrate, our strength, and our focus. Lastly, every ejaculation, whether through masturbation or conventional sex, has made us feel three times older than our actual age.

20

MASTURBATION

IN HIS BOOK TITLED *"The Virile Powers of Superb Manhood,"* Bernarr A. Macfadden expressed his thoughts on the subject of masturbation. The loss of physical manhood resulting from this one evil is horrible to contemplate.

The laws of sex should be as plain as the alphabet to every human being, even from early childhood. Boys grow up without a word said on this important subject. They come in contact with the most horrible and most destructive evils of life almost before the real struggle of life begins.

They enter it without a word of warning. "Masturbation outrages nature's sexual ordinances more than any or all the other norms of sexual sin man can perpetrate, and inflicts consequences the most terrible.

It is man's sin of sins, and vice of vices; and has caused incomparably more sexual dilapidation, paralysis, and disease, as well as demoralization, than all the other sexual depravities combined.

Neither Christendom nor heathendom suffers any evil at all to compare with this; because of its universality, and its terrible ravages on body and mind; and because it attacks the young idols of our hearts, and hopes of our future years. Pile all other evils together - drunkenness upon cheateries, swindlings, robberies, and murders; and tobacco upon both, for it is the greatest scourge.

All sickness, diseases and pestilences upon all; and war as the cap sheaf of them all - and all combined cause not a tithe as much human deterioration and misery as does this secret sin. "Private fornication causes twenty times more misery than any other sexual sin. And this is substantially the opinion of all who have examined this subject, including the creators of this blog.

The force of sexual energy reigns supreme in the vast expanse of the universe. The very substance that sparked your creation is also the very substance that propels your continuous growth and rejuvenation.

When one learns to harness sexual energy, they unlock a path to a life abundant in health, strength, prosperity, power, and godliness. This energy serves as the wellspring of vitality. Conversely, if this energy is squandered, the individual will experience depletion and weakness, marked by a lack of vigor and plagued by disease and imbalance.

Lust, undoubtedly, wields immense power as a weapon. It cunningly exploits your deepest carnal desires, leading you to squander your very essence. Consider this: a single sperm cell has the potential to give birth to an entirely new life!

And within you, there exist hundreds of millions of these cells. Can you fathom the benefits and potential of allowing your body to absorb such a vast reserve? What sort of individual would you transform into, possessing such boundless creative power?

In his book *Semen Retention: A Gentleman's Weapon for Superb Manhood, Self Help, Mental Health and Well Being*, Maldezin Rirnasqu had this to stay about the subject.

> **"Masturbation, also commonly known as self-abuse, is the greatest of all sexual evils, not only because of its widespread practice and the opportunity for excesses, but especially because of the fact that it generally works its harm during the period of growth, when the results of any sexual mistake or abuse are far more serious than they would be in adult life."**

The practice is detrimental at any phase of life, however, due to the drain upon the organism and the weakening or fatigue of the nerve centers which it implies. With semen retention, we recover our vitality and constitution one day at a time.

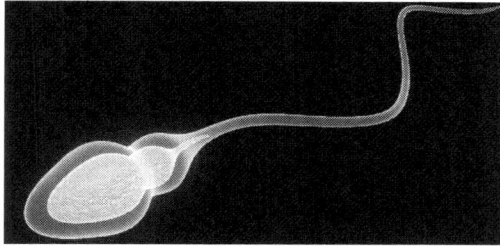

Masturbation is genuinely an assault against the body to such a degree that the ramifications are not just bodily, but moral or emotional as well. The mind and soul of the victim appear to be polluted at the same time as the body is weakened and sexual strength reduced by this horrible practice.

Masturbation is frequently regarded to be more detrimental to males than to girls, because of the direct drain upon the resources of the body in the case of the male via the loss of the seminal fluid.

But when one examines the destruction done upon the more fragile neurological systems of young women, it is not necessarily so obvious that they suffer less profoundly from the practice than do young males.

Naturally, the hurt that occurs from this specific evil is determined, to a very considerable amount, by two aspects, first the overall vital vigor of the sufferer, and second by the impacts on the complete bodily fabric.

The world is filled with young men and women suffering from the infirmities and mental tortures that accompany excessive early transgressions and screaming out, if I only had known, if I only had known.

I don't know how many thousands of letters I have received from men and women begging for assistance, most of them outlining the method in which they begun this habit, and declaring, in nearly all instances, that they had no notion that it was dangerous.

The secrecy on sex matters maintained by their elders had been such that they had had no opportunity to learn that it was wrong. This is why this channel provides you the knowledge of semen retention or abstinence, because the epidemic of masturbation has devastated countless lives.

The detrimental repercussions of masturbation are dual in type, the practice being first damaging to the sexual function itself, and second debilitating to the constitution. In other words, the behavior is unsexing on the one hand, and on the other hand, tends to erode the vigor of the body generally.

It would be impossible to state that each sort of weakness preceded the other, given circumstances differ. As a rule, the two findings go side by side. The fact that a man may survive an event does not indicate that it has been beneficial for him, or without harmful repercussions.

Many authors of the current day are clearly doing tremendous damage by dismissing the repercussions of self-abuse. They have so much to say about the exaggerations of the early authors, that the readers likely to acquire the sense that the habit is not that detrimental after all, and therefore does not strive to stop it.

This is why many individuals would dispute the practice of semen retention until they become sick, or fail horribly on their work, or have marital issues. They will then have to go within, and recognize that the issue arises from their bad practice of masturbation, or the excessive flow of the seminal fluid.

The reality is that masturbation is always damaging, even in the most minor degree, and when taken far, is exceedingly destructive. If not began until after mature years, then the outcomes will be less severe.

Unfortunately, however, it is done, in almost all instances, before the age of 18 years, more typically from 14 to 16, and sometimes it is kept up from the age of 12 or 14 till marriage, and sometimes even beyond that.

It is really true that when practiced extensively in the early years of youth, the results are often almost serious enough to justify the horrible pen pictures painted by the sensational and exaggerating writers of a generation ago, and even in adult life it is sufficiently debilitating, robbing a man of his bodily energies, his mental strength, his spirit, and his ambition, besides weakening the sex function itself, and inducing a condition of general unfitness for marriage.

It is a significant subject, especially in adult life. It is good to note too, that certain constitutions appear to be much stronger than others in this sense, and can bear considerably more abuse, just as some men can handle more alcohol and tobacco without displaying the immediate symptoms, even if these poisons are perpetually hurting them.

There are others who declare that masturbating never caused them any damage, thus they swiftly overlook the advantages of semen retention. The guy thinks this way about it, was presumably blessed by nature with great sexual power, but I don't believe this can ever be genuinely acknowledged.

I cannot concur with those who claim that it is only the excess that is detrimental. This habit is dangerous, no matter with what moderation it may be engaged in, just as alcohol and nicotine, even in tiny doses, are hazardous, in spite of the fact that the user may not be able to detect the consequences immediately.

The reality is that masturbation is constantly weakening and devitalizing, either in adolescence or in adult life. It is a procedure of completing gradually what castration achieves immediately.

It entails the steady eroding of masculinity and everything that goes with it. That the damage is sometimes overstated is probably true, but in light of the fact that the practice, when pursued far enough, entirely unfits a man for marriage and for life, any effort to diminish its significance may be criminally false.

The fact that the sufferer may still be able to dress himself and go about and eat, does not necessarily suggest that he is a man. Let the young guy who finds himself completely impotent ask some of these doctors what they mean by suggesting that the behavior is not very dangerous.

What is known as prematurity or premature ejaculation, a condition which is almost as bad as full impotence in disqualifying the sufferer for marriage, is one of the most prevalent of the outcomes of masturbation in males.

There are of course varying degrees of prematurity, ranging from a moderate instance to an extreme sensitive ness or hair trigger condition, in which the ejaculation may take place with little excitation or even before initiating the connection.

More or less premature ejaculation is generally the outcome when masturbation has been performed, to any meaningful amount, such as routinely perusing pornographic materials. In due time the masturbator trains his body to attain orgasm without the penetration that happens in intercourse.

A frequent misunderstanding concerning semen retention is that it promotes premature ejaculation, this is entirely false. A semen retention practitioner has closed his valve in comparison to a tap in contrast to the masturbator who has consistently conditioned his body to have an open valve.

Masturbation tends to exhaust the nerve centers of the spine, it also produces such a congestion of the various organs and glands of the reproductive system and taxes their strength to such an extent as to cause varicoccal, prostate enlargement and urethral inflammation, especially of the posterior urethra, possible atrophy of the testicles or other parts.

The general bodily effects of masturbation, apart from the effect on the generative system itself, are to be seen in a lack of energy or general lassitude, a weakened muscular system, an all around lack of development, sometimes a dragging gait, weakness of the bladder or urinary symptoms, a pale or sallow complexion often with dark rings around the eyes as well as pimples and blackheads, poor memory, difficulty in study or mental concentration, lack of self-confidence, a tendency to avoid the society of others, especially that of the opposite sex, and an inability to look other people in the eye.

On the other side, semen retention replenishes our skin and eyes, giving us that shine that many attest to. The mental or psychic symptoms are extremely essential and may be experienced in varied degrees.

A naturally strong-minded individual may overcome some of these, like for instance the lack of confidence by force of will, but in many situations these antisocial characteristics are quite apparent.

Weakened memory and impaired mental attention are among the most chronic and prevalent of such symptoms. The physical look does not, however, usually imply addiction to this habit, contrary to the comments of some of the ancient literature.

When the person has inherited great vitality, his inherent strength may allow him to tolerate severe abuse without displaying it visibly, so that we cannot, as a rule, determine by appearances.

21

CONQUERING THE HABIT

THE ESSENTIAL ISSUE IS, how may the habit be conquered? Following that comes the issue, how may one overcome the weakness coming from it, because we will have to deal, not only with the actual habit, but with the many abnormalities of the generative system which it leaves behind.

The restorative methods must be of a double nature, physical and mental. It would be impossible to determine which of these is the more significant aspect of the therapy because both are extremely vital.

In the first place, the building up of physical vitality is important. Not just for its own sake, but for the sake of the stronger mind that will arise from it, and which is vital for the struggle against this evil.

Semen retention or abstinence has been proved as a method that boosts testosterone levels, hence giving a basis for physique growth. Strength of will and intellect, you will discover, are difficult to develop in a badly functioning body with an insufficient blood supply to the brain and a broken-down system of nerves.

One should consequently do all necessary to promote muscular vitality and strength. The more closely you may achieve to a physique properly developed in other aspects, the more possibility you may have of restoring your sexual power.

Take pride in your physique and its strength. Build yourself up as closely as possible into the state of an athlete by varied sports exercises in the open air that are suitable to your strength and physical capabilities.

Keep in mind that maximizing the growth of any biological element is most effectively done by boosting the quality of blood and stimulating greater circulation. Therefore, adding workouts and holistic measures targeted at reinforcing the overall constitution is vital in reducing the impacts of self-abuse.

When practicing semen retention, the food is vital and should be non-stimulating in nature. Meat and eggs should not be used too freely and in a few tough cases in which the assimilation is extremely poor it would be best to avoid them completely.

The red foods are extremely stimulating and disagreeable in certain situations, while they may be useful in a case of impotence. Accumulations in the colon naturally pushing onto the prostate and crowding the other structures in such a manner as to induce agitation of the parts or at least to exacerbate it.

Therefore, the bowel should be maintained open and regular, there should be no irritation of the components via an over-distended colon. So far as the mental therapy of masturbation is concerned, the first important prerequisite is to come into the struggle with the unfaltering decision that you are going to quit the habit and then stick to it until you have done so.

The second requirement is to quit thinking about it and the third is to become so busy filling your life with so many types of mental activity that the old habit will not have any time to express itself or to concern you.

Your mind must be so engaged with other tasks that there will be no chance for lingering on licentious ideas. The fourth criterion is to avoid being too much alone yourself and to nurture the society of sophisticated people just as much as you reasonably can.

If the habit has taken a firm grip, you may be saddened to learn that in spite of your best intentions, you have been unable to break from its bondage. This is a frequent predicament for folks who have been hooked to this behavior for a time.

Don't become disillusioned by occasional failures. Instead, each time, begin afresh with even deeper desire to eliminate the habit and develop both physical strength and mental stamina. This will make it simpler for you to succeed.

Remember why you began the practice of semen retention. Remember that each time you reject the temptation, you are helping to build the habit of resistance. Each time you grow in the capacity to resist, and even if you may backslide periodically, nevertheless by consistently rejecting the desire and fighting the good fight, you will eventually build the strength of willpower that will allow you to abandon the practice totally.

Cultivate pride and self-respect. Hold up your head. Make people respect you. No matter what your task may be, even if it is merely study of some type, make up your mind that you will accomplish the best that can be done.

In that manner, you will acquire the respect of others as well as of yourself. The psychological influence of your attitude toward people is a major factor. Anything that will tend to add to your sense of pride will help you powerfully.

A nice chest will do more than anything in the way of apparel to give you pride. If you develop a physique that you can be proud of, you will be less motivated to mistreat it. Mental activity is the finest thing in the world by which to battle either this habit or any other.

Idleness is the huge insurmountable impediment. If you have nothing to do, find something. Inactivity will offer your mind an opportunity either to linger upon sensual ideas or to worry about your situation, and both of these should be carefully avoided.

One of the most successful tactics when presented with the temptation of the old habit is to instantly immerse oneself in the company of others whenever possible.

Minimize lonely time and be careful of the psychological ramifications of masturbation, which include lowering self-confidence, promoting shyness in social interactions, and inducing a predisposition to avoid others, especially those of the opposite sex. This remark highlights that the behavior is not merely a breach against bodily well-being, but also represents a spiritual and moral affront.

CONCLUSION

By simply observing the current state of the world, one can unmistakably perceive an ancient dark agenda at play. Corruption, debt, war, and orchestrated events are running rampant, leaving no room for doubt.

Humanity finds itself embroiled in a profound struggle for its soul and consciousness. The very institutions and governments that should protect us have been turned against us, manipulating our desires and ensnaring us in a web of addiction. By keeping our focus on our primal instincts, symbolized by the lower three chakras, they hinder our spiritual evolution.

Throughout history, ancient philosophies, religions, mystery schools, and spiritual groups have all provided clues on how to achieve liberation. Their message was clear: we must transcend our base desires, particularly lust.

There are those who doubt the health benefits of masturbation and semen loss during conventional sex. However, ancient teachings frequently advocated for celibacy and sex magic.

Based on research and personal experience of overcoming addiction to masturbation and porn, it is apparent that excessive masturbation and semen loss can result in degeneration of the mind, body, and soul. In contrast, retention and sexual alchemy are viewed as generative practices.

One gram of DNA holds over 200mmillion gigabytes (GB) of data. This advanced system of living information gives you the capabilities that you have. Only a few know that minerals play an integral role in DNA activation, and that the human body cannot access abilities inside the DNA without an ample supply of minerals. Genetically modified and minerals depleted food supply and porn are part of a plan to keep you in a weakened state, so the other 10 DNA strands won't be activated.

The word weakened sounds phonetically like the word weekend. How does humanity feel after the first five days of the week working and giving their life force energy to the CORPorations? -WEAKENED. That's why the last two days of the week are called a weekend/ weakened. The English language is very, very tricky and it is not a coincidence. The best weapon they have to dumb down society (especially men), is through "pornography". If you are a woman and think that if most men lose by wasting the golden mine (semen) that you don't have to worry, you are wrong. You lose too. First you lose the protector.

Do not be naive and think that you are independent, and you don't need men, as you do need men just as much as men need you. All the emasculation of man is done to take away their protection off you. The fabricated (man-made) laws are created as such to deceive you and think that you don't need men. Many women rely on the state for protection. But I ask you: Who does the state (government) protect you from? Men? A concrete proof that the government doesn't care about women is the fact that they want to jab (inject poison) men and women and children. Since I'm writing this book in the middle of the pLandemic had to use this example.

Let's assume men are dangerous, who made them dangerous and how? The authorities made them, of course they didn't point the gun in their head. They introduced alcohol, drugs, guns, fake news, porn and so on. All these weaken the state of mind. When a man is not himself, he doesn't know what to do, where to go. In that case, women would be nurturing them. But they wouldn't as the damage has already been done, both genders are separated through mind control schemes. The damage I'm talking about is that of separation through racism, genders, social status, nationality etc. Men protect women, and women nurture men. They both need each other.

In the book _Gain Wisdom Through Practiced Knowledge_ by Rimias K. Neo, the author states:

A child deserves a strong father and not a weak one. The entire process from germ cell to mature sperm is around 70-74 days. How often people ejaculate in our decayed world? Every few days or even every day, multiple times a day. It is crazy if you think about it. How much life force has been thrown away from mindless ejaculations. Testosterone is significantly lower in the last decades. It takes about seven days without ejaculating for a man's testosterone levels to significantly increase, even up to 50%. Millions of men do not have any control over their sexual thoughts, their urges and overall, their energy. These men are toxic men (I was one of them).

After each ejaculation, a man loses minerals and vitamins equal to running 15-20 miles. He who saves his seed is a powerful man, worthy of a powerful divine woman. Save your semen/seed, overcome your greed/ desires. The quality relationship you have with SEX reflects the quality of the relationship you have with *God. Women are divine (as men are), their bodies are pure natural heavenly creation and not merely temporal *pleasure for your lustful urges.*

* **"God**" means the unseen, the void, the quantum fabric web of energy that holds everything together a.k.a. the SOURCE. If you associate the word God with religion, that's on you, assuming that you could neglect information based on a specific word that you could have a problem with.

That's why porn exists, to numb your brain and feelings out so that you are weakened, powerless, brainless where your masculinity is destroyed, therefore you destroy anyone you get together with, including your children. Do not waste one of the rivers of life which is "semen". The other river is your blood (menstruation for women=life force). If you fast regularly, your system should begin to balance, your energy/oxygen levels will return, therefore your rational mind will be back where you will make conscious decisions and not unfruitful, self-destructive unconscious ones. Also, meditation will help you get back the calmness of your mind, after all, the problems begin in the mind and end there. You are already full and complete.

If you have to empty your balls is like wanting to empty the whole self. It is impossible that semen is created to be ejected and wasted. There is no mistake in the human design/biology. Ejaculating is like throwing your life away. I'm speaking from experience. It took me years to regain back my divine masculinity. I was depleted for many years. Only after you practice semen retention you'll begin retaining your life force and live longer.

In Tao there is a golden rule [novice] of semen/sexual energy preservation where it describes how many days of retention there have to be between ejaculation. Based on your age you should retain more or less days. This is the first step, the second step is to not ejaculate for 74 [the time from germ to full maturity spermatozoa formation] days at a time, and the final step is to not ejaculate at all until your last breath.

Again, in the same book by Rimias K. Neo, he goes on and continues by saying this about the importance of retaining the life force:

> **When semen is saved (not ejaculated) from not having sex and/ or masturbation, it gets reabsorbed in the body. The brain's health improves greatly because semen is full of important nutrients that boost brain function. All the immense power of a man's semen and a woman's egg creates a child/another human. That's why semen is meant to not be wasted/ejaculated unless it is for intentionally procreating with loving and genuine intention with the right person**

that feels/thinks the same. The same applies for the eggs. Women must not menstruate. You'll read later on another chapter about MR (Menstruation/blood-eggs Retention).

"*If you want to destroy any nation without war, make adultery or nudity common in the young generation.*" - Kenneth Saladin

Bibliography - Chapters **17, 18, 19, 20** and **21** are based from the sources below

The Illusion Of Us by Mathew La Croix

Body Mind SOUL: As You Believe So Shall It Be by Saimir Kercanaj

Gain Wisdom Through Practiced Knowledge by Rimias K. Neo

Purity Is Power by Shiraz Hussain

The Virile Powers Of Superb Manhood by Bernarr A. Macfadden

Semen Retention: A gentlemen's weapon for superb Manhood, Self Help, Mental Health & Well Being by Maldezin Rirnasqu

PREVENTGENOCIDE2023.Org

WORLD HEALTH ORGANIZATION

MEN'S HEALTH MAGAZINE

22

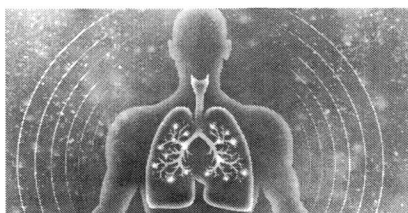

CHRIST CONSCIOUSNESS/
KUNDALINI AWAKENING

"Kundalini is the biological-psychological-spiritual mechanism driving human evolution, transforming humanity's consciousness, and making it possible for us to attain the tremendously expanded states of awareness, higher consciousness" - Gopi Krishna

ONE OF THE MANY REQUIREMENTS to activate the Kundalini is by breath meditation sessions. It is not difficult (the meditation) at all; all it needs is your time and your love for yourself and the world.

These things have them, for free, these were given to you since the moment that you were born. Make sure that you do this when there in a quite location if your house, so you don't get distracted by anything or anyone.

It takes only a few minutes a day either before or after a normal meditation session. The purpose of this meditation is to cause the **CFS** to travel down the spine so it can awaken the Kundalini.

> **What does CFS mean? CFS means CerebroSpinal Fluid or otherwise known as the 'Chrism Oil' or 'The Water of Life'. Deep conscious breathing practice, ionizes the CSF and causes the Kundalini to rise. The Kundalini needs food, and this magnetic, ionized powerful oil/substance feeds it. When it is fed, it feels alive and it moves upward the spine and into the pineal gland which causes the piezoelectric crystals of the pineal gland to be energized and this way the pineal gland fully opens up, the brain gets bathed in magnetized fluid, transforming you to Super Conscious or Christ Conscious being.**

This meditation has tremendous benefits. The chrism oil or the sacred secretion is the water of life. It will revitalize your body at a deep cellular level like you've never experienced before. The heart and the brain will be harmonized, it will be a coherence between the two as opposed to now where society lives in the rational deceptive mind. When this Kundalini awakens it will flood your whole body with super conscious energy, it will awaken also dormant neurons in the brain. It will elevate your light body (aura) and lymphatic water system. Your parasympathetic healing system (which governs healing, digestion and energetic clearance) will fully function. Your CSF will freely flow without any blockages, it's function will be boosted.

With an awakened Kundalini you will have visions, you could also develop remote viewing ability and many other psychic abilities. You can even move things with your mind. I have witnessed people moving objects without touching them. Movies have showed us many times this ability. Find a quiet place in the house or out in nature. Sit on the ground or on a carpet, pillow, or chair where your spine is nice and straight.

SEVEN MINUTES MEDITATION SESSION FOR AWAKENING YOUR KUNDALINI

STEP 1 - **INHALE** for 7 seconds (inhale by using all the capacity of your lungs, including your diaphragm) through your nose while visualizing a bright white light/energy from your crown going down the spine to the root charka, where the Serpent/Kundalini is laying dormant.

When you begin counting, open your heart, your shoulders must go back, arch, and chin slightly up. At the end of your 7 counts when you take all your breath in, you must engage the root triple lock steps by...**holding**...

HOLD for 7 seconds your breath while squeezing/contracting at the same time your:

(1) *Pelvis floor Muscles*

(2) *Perineum/Anus Muscles and*

(3) *Stomach Muscles*

While you hold your breath for 7 seconds in this triple root lock, your energy, will multiply, it will stir the Serpent/Kundalini energy that is coiled at your root.

In these 7 seconds that you are holding your breath, visualize that white light/energy that you previously brought down the spine from the crown chakra, visualize it in your root chakra as if it is getting even brighter and bigger like a giant diamond shining. After the 7 seconds of holding your breath...**exhale**...

STEP 2 - **EXHALE** through your mouth for the duration of another 7 seconds. While you exhale through the mouth curve your spine toward the front into a 'C' shape while your bring your arms on top of your thighs.

As you do this exhale, visualize that dazzling magnificent white light traveling back up the spine and to the crown. All this root triple lock and the circular motion of the spine will stimulate your cerebrospinal fluid and your kundalini nerves/energy (Ida, Pingala, and Sushumna). Your spinal cords floats in that living water (CFS). Water is life, most people use the words 'life' and 'alive' but they don't have any idea what truly being alive means.

Repeat this Inhale-Hold-Exhale practice for about 7 minutes by visualizing brilliant light for the whole duration of this meditation practice. It takes me about 20-30 seconds to feel the Kundalini. It must not be a challenge. Take your time. In my case I have been practicing meditating and creativity for a while. If you cannot visualize any bright light (with your eyes closed of course) then you must work on doing creative activities so that you are not predominantly a left brained individual.

The only right way to heaven is within, and is through your right side of the brain, which is responsible for creativity, nurturing, empathy etc. To know where exactly the diaphragm is, hold one hand two inches (5cm) away from your mouth, and the other hand on your belly where the belly button is. Pretend you are blowing out a candle, when you do this, you should feel with your other hand/palm the location of your diaphragm contracting a little bit. Most people are chest/short breathers.

You must practice taking full breaths, whether you are meditating or not. Also, to practice this meditation, your body and mind must be relaxed. You can't do this as soon as you finished a workout or if you were in an environment with lots of people shouting/talking or if you were listening to dance or heavy metal music. Your mind must be in Alpha brain wave, where you are relaxed.

Even better if you do this after a bath/shower. This inhale-hold-exhale mediation can even be in the backyard or anytime, anywhere as long as its quite outside and inside your mind. Practice this breathing technique not only when the Moon enters your zodiac sign (including practicing it every time there is a full moon), but also at other times. Meditation should be as normal as breathing is. From the book *Gain Wisdom Through Practiced Knowledge* by Rimias K. Neo

To turn lead into gold means to transmute your sexual energy, to not waste it but to use it to achieve enlightenment. Even though you become a little more enlightened every time you progress no matter how slow. To transmute this super powerful energy, you must raise the sacred secretion up to the brain, your electromagnetic/consciousness pilot. Everything begins and end in the mind. Use your thoughts to make the right choices where you rebuild as opposed to destroying yourself.

23

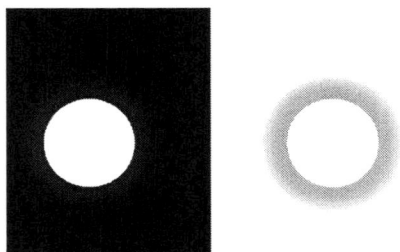

BALANCE THE FEMININE AND THE MASCULINE ENERGIES WITHIN YOURSELF IF YOU WANT TO RAISE THE MOTHER KUNDALINI

BOTH WOMEN AND MEN have masculine and feminine energies in them. There is a big difference between awaken and raising your kundalini. Anyone can awaken the kundalini (subtly or violently) but not everyone can raise it unless one properly balances both the masculine and the feminine energies in them.

DIVINE W O M E N
We are in the time of "revelation" and women are merely in touch with the pulse of this primordial instinct and greater "pole shift".

Women in general have lost touch with their inner divine feminine, which in turn cause men to completely be lost since only women can lead a man to his heart. The Goddess is revealing her form. The "Apocalypse" is the unveiling. Isis' veil is being removed.

As her veil thins, and her form is revealed, we are collectively re-discovering many secrets which have been hidden from us for several millennia!

This includes the origin of our species. "His-story" is going to become her-story as well, filling in the gaps where much has been obscured, revised and blatantly fabricated. The indigenous wisdom that has managed to prevail against all odds, throughout the period of colonization, will by the very nature of its content, develop the appropriate gravity to bring those whom the Ancestors have chosen, back into the orbit of their heritage and birthright.

We all have an indigenous past, on different timelines. We all have a unique culture and it's related traditions. I encourage you to learn about your ancestry if you have not, and to ask the Ancestors to guide you home to the truth of what you are. You might be surprised what you discover! I certainly was.

A large part of my tantric practice is dedicated to Ancestral Veneration. As someone disconnected from familial ties and land of origin, this was such an abstract and triggering concept to me as someone who experienced a great deal of abandonment trauma from my family of origin.

I found that my practice could only go so deep, as long as I was unwilling to connect with my ancestors. It was necessary to go back beyond the known, in order to find a bridge to traverse that did not include the pain of the present state of my familial relations as these were blockages to any progress.

Finally, I surrendered and asked the Ancestors to show me who they were. And that took me on a most wonderful journey of exploration into the past with many unexpected and surprising twists and turns. The connection has been restored, I know where I come from and who I am.

My version of how it is that we got from point A to point Z in time, is now completely and utterly different than any explanation of history I've ever encountered in any public institution. These institutions seem to be strategic alliances whose objectives are to maintain a mass delusion, in order to prevent the restoration of ones spiritual inheritance.

*Should you be so inclined to dig further, you can learn about admiralty/maritime law. We are split into a duality through the formation of a decedent (dead) estate. This is used to engage in commerce within the jurisdictions of systems that have been overlayed upon the natural world, that is what colonization is.

Again, the Mother, or matter - which is the Goddess, does not recognize any arbitrary boundary or jurisdiction AT ALL.

She has imbued us with a Godly Estate and only recognizes Natural Law as true law, not some man-made constructs designed to turn humans into commodities on a market.* I also know it is no accident I am here at this very special time of transition. And you are too. I hope you will be able to experience this truth for yourself.

GIVE THE KEY TO YOUR CASTLE ONLY TO THOSE DESERVING IT

The divine woman is a goddess of the heart and a rebel of the soul. She will attract her king when she has healed her parts of pain and can fully open her heart to the **masculine**. She will attract her king because their souls reunite and a recognition of the soul takes place. As a result, the energy of the awakened **feminine** is reconnected with the energy of the **masculine** man.

This happens before any physical touch between the two connected souls. The recognition of souls only arises when the conscious **feminine** opens her heart to the awakened **masculine**.

"The Goddess knows exactly what she wants, and she waits
until a masculine presents his soul and opens his heart to her."
– Colin Enrico

He presents her with his compassion and feeling, and she is able to see his true nature. She knows that he can be emotionally balanced and put his ego aside. The God has gone inwards and faced his deep pain and processed them so well.

She will feel complete and safe when the masculine has opened his heart to her and can give her love from the depths of his soul.

Once both the awakened masculine and feminine pieces have healed, the healing process can proceed gradually. And they will heal each other automatically and sometimes unconsciously. This is because you can completely show yourself to each other, without putting on any masks.

The two souls are so connected that when they are separated they can feel empty without the other. This is due to the recognition of the soul and the unity of the two souls. In a healthy relationship it's always important that you can be good to yourself. And you can set each other free.

When the two souls look at each other, there is recognition of the two souls and they become connected.

When the two souls come close to each other and a touch takes place, you can feel each other's energy. It can be so strong that flames literally burst from it. Energetic electric currents flow like a serpent through the body.

The sexual feminine energy in the body is awakened, which in contemporary life is called "Kundalini energy".

If the masculine lives from his heart, he can even whisper her name to her, and she will hear his voice. The above was beautifully said by Colin Enrico.

DIVINE M E N

Men have lost their masculinity. Men have become children in grown up bodies. Men live in their mind which in turn creates emotional turmoil. Times have proved again and again that men have become further weakened from foods, drinks (alcohol) especially PORN. Even if you don't watch porn but masturbate or have sex many times or with different partners you are weakening your fortress. The mere fact of ejaculating your life essence, puts you in the back seat, chained with a million of bricks thrown over you.

We, as men, along with evolving ourselves, would do quite well to innerstand that the Sacred Women of this beautiful planet have been dominated, suppressed, manipulated, mistreated, disempowered, abused, neglected, silenced, and otherwise maligned for CENTURIES. These Magnificent Beings of the female persuasion are now breaking all those shackles and embracing their power and sovereignty. They carry a consensus group disdain for their long-term oppression. Our Loving Support of their much-awaited return to their Goddess Selves is needed as they find their way back to who they always were before it was stripped from them. Be patient, be flexible, and know that if you are a decent man with a good heart who cherishes her and lights her fires she will choose you. She might seem to be pulling away, but that is just her finding her crown of true Sovereignty. If you are falling short of being her choice, step it up a little. Go the extra mile, or five, or twenty.

She will notice and cherish you for showing her how worthy she is to you by your efforts and actions. Our role as men is honoring ourselves, and double honoring the finally free to be Radiant Divine Goddesses walking in our midst. Divine masculine will be feeling the strong shift in the energies. Their fear of being away from their feminine is surrounding them and they will be pushed to take physical action toward their feminine. Bad dreams, distance and longing for their divine Feminine is what is coming up and the righteous path will be clear to them.

Their Ego self will die, their intuition is going to make them take divine steps toward inner union. You must create a personal relationship with God by looking within. I'm pretty sure the divine masculine is aware of this. Sometimes us guys need to hear it in case our Divine masculine is distorted by the confusions of this crazy world. We all need healing. Say "no more" to being separated. We both need each other. We are each other.

The Divine Masculine is moving through an important upgrade. One that will help them see through the dark fog that had consumed them since the end of 2019. Rejection wounds from the Dark Mother that block receiving will come. You will also be looking at healing in a more focused manner as inner DM (Divine Feminine) is now waking up to the Source. It is all about receiving hence forth and you will inner stand what it means to accept yourself and heal the childhood trauma that has sabotaged the union between the Divine Feminine and the Divine Masculine energies. Any father issues that highlight abandonment and shame will also come up for reflection.

A tower moment regarding Sexuality will take place as wounds masquerading as False Projections will collapse. You will innerstand better who you are and you won't let Unconscious behavior in Karmic Timelines hurt you or the DF (Divine Feminine). You also may be guided to open Lines of Communications to express yourself. Expression means to practice alchemy, since everything id energy including how you express yourself. The quality of your thoughts and actions will determine how good of an alchemist you are. The road ahead is long.

Through sheer will power and discipline you can conquer your fears, worries and anything of low vibration that holds you a hostage. By balancing the feminine and masculine energies in you it doesn't mean to have 50% feminine and 50% masculine energies. If you are a man than you must be a 100% masculine while at the same time understanding your feminine side. When you understand your feminine side you will then understand women. Understanding your feminine side doesn't make you feminine.

One example, Women are much more nurturers and intuitive than men. But also, men are nurturers and intuitive. If you are by yourself with your child and your child gets hungry, you will cook or at least try to take care of the child as a mother would. Sure, you would not do as good of a job as the mother, but you would do it anyway because you have that feminine side in you. If you were not an empathetic and caring person at all, then you wouldn't be a human, you would be a monster, just as there are many monsters in this world. The above description applies the same for women. The woman too, can try and do the father for her child in the absence of the father. The point is that both women and men are made of feminine and masculine energies. Men are predominantly masculine; women are predominantly feminine. Each gender has their own strength and it's how it should be for a balance family/relationships/unions.

YIN	YANG
Feminine	Masculine
Internal Energy	External Energy
Yielding	Dominating
Nurturing	Initiating
Negative	Positive
Night	Day
Passive	Active
Moon	Sun
Intuitive	Logical
Cold	Hot
Soft	Hard

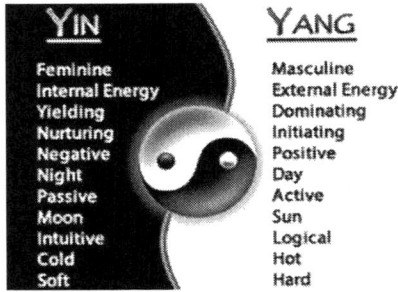

A lot of people feel like they need to find someone else to complete them. Nobody can complete you. You can only find completion within yourself. The purpose of mating (relationship) with someone, is to share your completeness. No such thing as 'the other half'. Well, if you cut an apple in half and give one half to your friend, he or she has the other half. But you are not an apple, are you? You are a living conscious sentient being, you are full, complete, you are whole. An apple is also living organism, but that's not what we're talking about here. Unless you realize this, you'll always chase a fictional "*the other half*".

The best relationship you can have is the one with yourself. You must realize and live in sacred intimacy with yourself first before you attract those that will compliment (not complete) you. In the movie "Rocky 3", when Rocky told his coach that he couldn't beat the opponent, among other things, Rocky's trainer Micky told Rocky that he got civilized, that's what happened. By "civilized" he meant that he got married, had a child and became a part of the herd mentality/society. Before Rocky had a child, he was strong as a bull. When he became a family man, he did not have that strength in his heart to really fight anymore. The point is that Rocky had lost that intimacy that he had with his true self, with who he truly was, he had become civilized.

A man's legs become weak by a woman, meaning that a man loses his mind when he satisfies his base desires. At one point in this movie or in the previous one, in Rocky 2, Rocky's wife told him to not fight anymore. Fighting is what Rocky was good at. Then Rocky told her: "I never asked you to stop being a woman so please don't ask me to not be a man".

The reason why I'm writing about the part of the movie mentioned above, is to point out that many people get into a relationship before developing first a strong relationship with themselves. There are also cases when people lose that relationship with themselves after a few years of being married or in a relationship. This is mostly men that fall after they get married. If you were a strong man when you got together with her, you will have to remain strong until the last breath. She wants a strong man. Just as men are attracted to women that fully honor their feminine divine selves, so are women attracted to men that fully honor their masculine divine selves.

> "He who wastes his essence away on a regular
> basis will have no elixir left to live."

<u>Bibliography</u>

I AM The Key That Opens All Doors by Saimir Kercanaj

Gain Wisdom Through Practiced Knowledge by Rimias K. Neo

You Are The One by Pine G. Land

24

LIBERTY TREE – ALLOW YOUR KUNDALINI TO BECOME FREE

In 1775, in the ballad "Liberty Tree", Thomas Paine wrote:

---

*In a chariot of light, from the regions of day,
the **Goddess of Liberty** came, ten thousands
celestials directed her way, and hither conducted
the dame. A fair budding branch from the
garden above, where millions with millions
agree, she brought in her hand as a pledge of her
love, and the plant she named **Libert Tree**.*

WHAT THOMAS PAYNE WROTE, has absolutely nothing to do with Kundalini, his poetry was about liberty/freedom, even though metaphorically/allegorically one can relate it to the Kundalini if one wants to, since the awakening and the raising of the Kundalini means FREEDOM. I used this poem here because I liked some words such as "Liberty Tree, garden above, plant etc." The tree is your spine, the garden is your opened pineal gland a.k.a. the Garden of Eden. A chariot of Light is your Merkaba or Light Body Vehicle when the kundalini is fully raised and all your chakras are opened and balanced. You cannot chain the gate to freedom.

Every action, emotion and thought that you experience in life is like experiencing the tree (roots, trunk, branches, leaves, fruit-color/smell/taste). Life is full of wonderful things such as plants, trees, the sun, the sky, rivers/oceans all the way the interactions you have with people and animals. Most people are not free because they want more than they actually need, they do not understand that earth is full of abundance, we are full of abundance.

Real abundance is priceless, it cannot be bought with money. You may say "but we need money to survive". No, we don't need any money if we unite together and care about one another. See, money is not the problem, the intention behind it is the problem. Money is just energy like everything else. We are alchemists, we direct the energy in whichever way we want, consciously or unconsciously. People, in general work long hours daily to buy and consume things they don't need. They have been conditioned to think that those things they purchase would bring them happiness but no matter how much you earn and consume, you'll never find happiness out there.

Happiness is within yourself. The kundalini energy which is part of your nervous system will thrive or remain stagnant or dormant based on your daily actions or inactions. Usually we use the term "awakened or not awakened kundalini". Kundalini is already awake, had it not been awake our Central Nervous system would not be working. Hence, the very energy that runs our CNS is Kundalini, also it's energy extends to the peripheral nervous system, and beyond. By "Kundalini awakening" it generally means awakening it even more than usual, for example a wire carrying 220V electricity is already a live wire, however for greater purposes 440V electricity may be required. Similarly for higher states of Spiritual realisation, for deeper states of meditation etc.

Kundalini is required to be awakened even more, but prior to that there are preparatory yogic practices for being ready enough for that energy, just as the wirings and machinery needs to be modified to suit 440V electricity.

Generally, one has to engage in yogic practices under the guidance of a Guru/Spiritual Master who him/herself has awakened kundalini and knows about it by first hand experience, as there may be certain psychological changes and/or changes in life altogether after someone awakens the Kundalini, and then it is of utmost importance to be counselled and guided by the Guru, because only he/she knows about all the effects/side effects of such awakening. For many people their kundalini awakened by itself without any practice. For some the kundalini awakening is violent and to others is awakened without any major discomfort.

**You are the tree of knowledge. We are all going through
a remembering transition period. Slowly, but surely
we are remembering who we truly are.**

Kundalini can get awakened by intense thoughts/emotions too, but to keep it awake, or manage it's energy one needs to know the actual yogic processes, as thoughts may also lead to imagination/ fabrication. If you are a self-aware person, you can be your own Yogi/ teacher/master. A lot of people need a hand in being put in the right direction and that's where other teachers come in but as always, you are the ultimate teacher. You can read books or talk to people, but in the end it is you that must make decisions about your life. There are very few people who may have had spontaneous or miraculous Kundalini awakenings, however that's not the general way of chronologically awakening Kundalini, so those are exceptional happenings.

Kundalini awakening, is the beginning of a much larger Spiritual journey, hence just awakening the Kundalini is not the final goal/ final achievement, the final goal is Nirvana, which is a goal and not a goal at the same time. What does a goal and not a goal at the same time means? To achieve something, you must have a goal, and to reach that goal you have to develop discipline. Without willpower and determination, you cannot develop a disciplined character/ personality. Knowledge is vast, we must practice knowledge so that it becomes wisdom. Knowledge unpracticed is useless, not only useless but it can also be harmful in the hands of people with bad intentions and in the hands of people that lack knowledge of self. In other words, knowledge is practiced properly and for good intentions by self aware open-minded and open-hearted people.

One (out of many) thing that prohibits the kundalini awakening or that causes a violent kundalini awakening is ATTACHMENTS, especially fear of losing something or someone. Fear of loss stems from attachment. We cling to people, possessions, and even ideas, believing that they define our happiness and identity. This attachment can lead to anxiety, stress, and a perpetual state of unease, as the fear of losing what we value looms over us. By training ourselves to let go, we are not dismissing the importance of these things but rather shifting our perspective on their role in our lives. You mind is limited as to how many operations it can handle daily.

If you spend your time listening to many people's opinions daily, you will overload your brain, your consciousness and all that will create a short circuit and you will even make mistakes in things that usually are basic knowledge. Practicing solitude is of utmost importance. Only in solitude you can finally be with yourself. The more you talk/speak about something, the more you hang around with people you will develop attachment to them. You must detach from them; they are their own selves. So, you too must become your own self again.

Detachment does not mean indifference. Instead, it means acknowledging the transient nature of all things. Everything in life is impermanent – relationships, material possessions, and even our own existence. By accepting this, we learn to appreciate the present moment without the constant dread of future loss. This mindset fosters gratitude and allows us to experience life more fully. Moreover, letting go cultivates emotional resilience. When we are not shackled by fear, we can face life's challenges with a clearer mind and a steadier heart. We become adaptable, able to navigate changes and losses with grace. This resilience is crucial for personal growth, as it empowers us to move forward without being paralyzed by fear or regret. The biggest shackles are invisible/mental. What you can't see is more powerful than what you can see.

Practicing detachment also enhances our relationships. When we let go of the fear of losing loved ones, we can love them more freely and authentically, without the shadow of possessiveness or anxiety. This creates healthier, more fulfilling connections based on mutual respect and trust. Countless of relationships have been destroyed as a result of one of the partner's fear in losing the other one. How can you be scared to lose someone if they are not yours to begin with? Everyone is temporary in your life. Only you will be will you until the end of this temporary incarnation (prison or paradise). Fear of losing someone stems from low self-esteem, from not knowing who you truly are. If you are scared to lose someone, then you are affirming to be weak. And as the law of manifestation goes, you will attract weakness in your life, or strength if you are strong mentally and emotionally.

In practical terms, letting go requires mindfulness and self-awareness. Meditation, reflection, and conscious practice of gratitude can help shift our mindset. By focusing on the present and recognizing the impermanence of life, we train ourselves to release our grip on fears and attachments. Ultimately, embracing this principle leads to a more serene, resilient, and enriched life. It frees us from the bondage of fear, allowing us to live with greater courage, joy, and wisdom. You are the tree of knowledge. Realize this and you will **REBUILD YOURSELF FROM WITHIN.**

We hope you found this book useful and empowering. Our intention was and will always be to never stop fighting for freedom. We will not stop until humanity becomes free once and for all. We appreciate your time and effort in working on yourself so that you can become the leader of your life and shine the light on the right path so that others will be empowered by YOUR example.

Consider spending a few moments and review this book on Amazon.

WE THANK YOU
FROM THE DEPTHS OF OUR HEARTS

J.J and Tamo

RESOURCES

1- *KNOWLEDGE OF THE HIGHER WORLDS AND ITS ATTAINMENT by* **Rudolf Steiner**

2- *YOU ARE NOT A STRAWAN YOU ARE THE ZYGOTE* by **Saimir X. Kercanaj**

3- *Saint Germaine on ALCHEMY FORMULAS FOR SELF-TRANSFORMATION by* **Mark L. Prophet**

4- *Gain Wisdom Through Practiced Knowledge* by **Rimias K. Neo**

5- *YOU ARE THE ONE* by **Pine G. Land**

6- *ALKALINE PLANT BASED DIET by* **Aqiyl Aniys**

7- *KUNDALINI THE SACRED FIRE OF ALL RELIGIONS by* **Samael Aun Weor**

8- *CONNECTING WITH THE ARCTURIANS* by **David K. Miller**

9- *SAMADHI Unity Of Consciousness and Existence* by **Ivan Antic**

10- *ELECTRIC BODY ELECTRIC HEALTH by* ***Eileen Day McKusick***

11- *The Warrior's Meditation* by ***Richard L. Haight***

12- *I Am The Key That Opens All Door by Saimir Kercanaj*

13 - *Semen Retention: A gentlemen's weapon for superb Manhood, Self Help, Mental Health & Well Being* by **Maldezin Rirnasqu**

14 - *Purity Is Power* by **Shiraz Hussain**

15 - *The Virile Powers Of Superb Manhood* by **Bernarr A. Macfadden**

16 - *The Order of The Gnostics* by **Mr. Moe Bedard**

17 - *The Mystery of Golden Flower* by **Samel Aun Weor**

18 - *Practical Astrology* by **Samael Aun Weor**

19 - *Treatise of Sexual Alchemy by* **Samael Aun Weor**

https://www.chakras.info
https://interestingliterature.com/
www.thejoywithin.org

For a lot more recommended books check the website below:
https://theserpentsway.com/recommended-books/

Printed in Great Britain
by Amazon

54416384R00124